THE LITTLE GIRL INSIDE

Owning My Role in My Own Pain

Tonya Barbee

The Little Girl Inside
Owning My Role In My Own Pain
All Rights Reserved.
Copyright © 2017 Tonya Barbee

This book is a work of non-fiction based on the life, experiences and recollections of the author and not of the publisher. All names have been changed to protect the privacy of others. The author has stated to the publishers that, except in such respects, not affecting the substantial accuracy of the work, the contents of this book are true.

This book may not be reproduced, transmitted, or stored in whole or in part by any means, including graphics, electronic, or mechanical without the express written consent of the publisher except in the case of brief quotations embodied in critical articles, reviews or broadcasts.

I'm Still A Rose™ Books

ISBN: 0999670603
ISBN 13: 9780999670606

Cover Photography by style2photography All rights reserved – used with permission.
Cover Design by Tywebbin Creations, LLC

PRINTED IN THE UNITED STATES OF AMERICA

Tonya Barbee

To my children. It started with you.

My grandbabies, you ignite my entire being!

CONTENTS

Acknowledgments — ix
Special Thanks — xiii
Foreword — xv
Preface — xvii

1	Dreams	1
2	Foundation	3
3	Starry Eyes	5
4	Open Eyes	6
5	Weary Eyes	8
6	Lessons	10
7	Denial	12
8	Lost	15
9	Fast Forward	17
10	A Blast from my Past	19
11	A Breath of Fresh Air	21
12	Love and Technology	23
13	Again	27
14	And Again	33
15	Seeing Red	38
16	Honeymoon	40
17	Taking the Lead	43

18	Looking Glass	46
19	Repeat Performance	49
20	New Routine	52
21	Make it Better	55
22	Fragile Trust	57
23	Unsettlement	61
24	Returns and Regrets	64
25	Nail in the Coffin	73
26	Retreat	78
27	Sigh of Relief	85
28	Owning It!	87

What's Happening Now?	91
About the Author	93

ACKNOWLEDGMENTS

Inspirations:

First and foremost, I thank God for picking me up every time I fell and giving me the strength to never give up. My daddy, the Major. Daddy, I acquired your strength. I know you are lookng down on us. Ma, alias Mo-Mo, my mother, thank you for all the support throughout these years, helping me with the kids while I went out in the world to explore every opportunity; you were always there to hold the fort down. I thank my sisters for their support.

Uncle Rockie, alias Rock Tipton, in your other life you were a comedian AND a therapist. You kept me in line and out of some serious trouble. You "so rock!" I love you. Rev. Barbara Harmon (deceased); Dr. Louis Kelly; Rev Gwen Sutton; Rev. Sheila Bender; Bishop Joel Njoku; Pastor Henry P. Davis, III; Rev. Carol Lambert; Rev. Melony Taylor; Cousin/Rev Amantha Barbee, and Rev. Delores Davis.

How can I lose when surrounded by this wealth of spiritual knowledge? Each of you has had a tremendous impact in my life – your powerful sermons, stern advice, and even admonishments. I am still growing as a result. Ms. Pierotti and Ms. Foreman, thank you, because you inspired me to write and act. You laid the foundation. I never forgot anything you taught me at Ballou H.S. It's never too late to implement the plan. Elaine Muir, I watched and I learned so much from you, the work-lessons. You still inspire me, even over fifteen years later after working with you.

Dr. Joyce Hamilton Berry, my former therapist, (only because of retirement) you taught me to look beyond potential and ask myself, "Can you live with this person today?" I thank the Lett family for their support. Sherronne Battle, thank you; your lifelong friendship. Thank you for looking at every page of this book, no matter how you felt.

Dawne Easley Clairborne, your friendship of over forty years is solid as a rock! Thank you for being there when I really needed you and for always keeping it real. Jackie Chandler, girl, you are a powerhouse! You lead, I follow. Dr. Francis Ponti, your mentorship for over twenty years was inspirational! I now understand everything that you shared with me. Thank you for believing in me. Melissa Dent, Angela Alexander, Crystal Simpkins, Pat Mitchell, and Angela Alexander of the Spiritual Gangstas - the strength of Job! Michael Mann, my big brother, so inspirational. You inspire me, challenge me, and coach me. You are the man! Thanks for being there, my mentor, 24/7. Kenneth Cunningham, a friend for life! You've been there through it all and I'll never forget you for it. Thank you for believing in me. Rick Appia, you kept it real. I won't forget our discussions. Gary Bolden, you keep me laughing and thank you for helping me to get to the bottom of it. You were there through a very tough time. Amazing! I actually still have the notes from our long conversations and all of your advice.

Conway Vance and David Cousins, thank you for the retreats on your beautiful boats. It inspired me more than you will ever know. Thank you for treating me like a queen when I needed it the most!

Attorneys and team from Robert Aides and Associates, I thank you for saving my life. Without your firm's support, it would not have been a smooth process. Attorney Aides, thank you for making time for me. I won't ever forget you. Mr. Rite and Mr. Price, you're awesome! You treated me like I was a millionaire! I appreciate each of you. And Mr. Darrell Robinson, you too.

Each of you has truly inspired me. Thanks for letting me talk your ears off, never missing a beat, while giving me so much clarity and direction and most importantly, your precious time.

Thank you ALL for touching my life in a powerful way.

"We must find time to stop and thank the people who make a difference in our lives." -John F. Kennedy

SPECIAL THANKS

My friend and colleague Dr. Lesia Banks for coaching me how to take control of my own story, my life. My graphic designers and web team, especially Mike Jacobs, Ty Moody, and photographers Katherine Lewis and style2photography. I appreciate everything you're doing and going to do. The "I am Still a Rose™" team will empower many lives. My bosses and coworkers for their support during my journey. Jose Torres, thank you for helping me find loads of research material. Mary Bowser, your support during this journey will never be forgotten. Bruce Lewis, your friendship is immeasurable! And, you kept me smiling.

Dr. Stan Boddie thanks for the spiritual mentoring. I truly needed the encouraging words. Adrienne Ferguson, thank you for the beautiful dresses. Donna Powers, your thoughtfulness is amazing! How do you have the energy? Thank you for always brightening my days at work with your giving spirit and a heart of gold. Last, but certainly not least, my partner, Teddy. You have been incredibly supportive through this project and all of my other dreams as well. Teddy Froneberger, I love you with all my heart! I thank you for believing in me even more than I had once believed in myself. Hand, Fist/chest!

FOREWORD

What an absolutely powerful, courageous, and inspirational work Tonya has produced! I was com- pletely captivated and riveted by Tonya's remarkable story of perseverance and faith to deal with challenging, life- changing personal situations. Each of us will have our own chal- lenges, and many of us will experience similar instances of critical, life-changing situations. The questions for all of us are: How do we deal with these situations and, more importantly, what will we learn from them? Tonya bravely bares her soul in telling her story, sharing extraordinary faith, perseverance, and commitment to remain the person that God has called her to be, rather than letting obstacles dictate who she is in life.

Tonya's book is a brilliant reflection of situations many people find themselves in today, and deals frankly with real-life circumstances. Many of us have a "Little Girl" or a "Little Boy" inside of us. Tonya reminds us that we must think carefully about how we respond to that little person. This book is a "must read" for young adults as well. I thank God for instilling his voice in Tonya and for filling her with a message of faith and hope. I encourage everyone who reads this book to reflect on God's greatness, and to consider how God can enable us to deal with whatever circumstances and situations we may confront in life.

-Dr. Stan Boddie

PREFACE

Before I decided to write this book, I asked myself over and over again, "How on earth did I get myself into one bad relationship after another?" As I wrote, the answer became clear. Oftentimes, we allow the little child inside of us to dictate what we should do, and whom we should do it with. We have to admit, we see many warning signs as we are pon- dering decisions, but we ignore the signs. We are warned not to choose certain paths, but we skip, hopefully, along them anyway. We allow the child inside to take over, and sometimes, it makes it easier to live with the decisions we've made as well. We convince ourselves that the path we choose to take will not present danger or challenges. There's a complex conversation taking place in our hearts and minds that's occasionally hard to control. Wisdom sees the pitfalls and the consequences. The starry-eyed child, however, sees what could be and ignores what is.

It was therapeutic for me to explore the reasons behind my repetitive bad choices and resulting bad circumstances. It didn't take consultation with a professional for me to realize that the dizzying cycle had to be broken. Only I had to take control of my life to break the negative cycle. It was my responsibility. Four failed marriages demanded that I get answers. I felt I had no choice but to write about the fourth, because the subsequent suffering began to consume me.

It was difficult to acknowledge, but I began to see patterns. I had to take responsibility for my circumstances.

My goal is to help others who have faced similar issues. It is unacceptable to justify any poor decision, and the multitude of consequences that come as a result of poor choices can always be avoided. It is my hope that as you read this, you will see that moving forward happily and honestly demands a sober look at past decisions. Reality can't be explained away or ignored. It must be faced boldly with accountability and conviction.

No one is sure who coined the phrase, "It is what it is," but sometimes that attitude of acceptance is the best response to circumstances that cannot be altered. However, when we *can* do something about correcting or improving our circumstances, we should use every available tool to do so. We have to deal with reality, my friends. Words are wonderful but *action*, however, is even more formidable. Action!

I've learned to take my time in relationships. I now understand how critical it is to get to know people. Instincts, discernment, and intuition aren't sinister, they are valuable and I've learned to trust mine. I like the little girl inside me, but she can't be at the helm of my life. The blame game is over. My pain demands that I acknowledge my role in its existence. That is the first step to erasing it and leading an authentic life.

1

DREAMS

Is there a little girl who doesn't grow up dreaming of the day a knight in shining armor will come and sweep her off her feet? She's in a fairy tale world. The little girl is waiting for her Knight in Shining Armor to protect her, care for her, and love her forever. He is faithful, loyal, and courageous. He will fight for her and protect her from all evil.

The little girl, in a make-believe world, grown up, looking for her Knight in Shining Armor.

She wanted it all: education, career, independence. and to be taken care of protected, and adored. It is her right. It is her purpose in life. That's what she had always been told. She does not play with her dolls, she raises them; nurtures them as if they are real. She is practicing. Her knight will protect her and provide for her and the babies. In exchange, she will give love, love, and more love. It's oozing out of every pore. It's what she's made of. It's better than food and water, who needs that as long as she has her Knight and Shining Armor anyway.

Love and be loved. That's the goal. Some fine stranger from afar has his eye on her. Of all of the female human beings on earth, she is the chosen one. She waits patiently because he's going to race to her street on his trusty steed, or some other mode of dashing, fairy-tale transportation, and take her to La-La Land on the corner of Happily-Ever-After and Heavenly Bliss. That's the plan. Sing, "Twinkle, Twinkle, Little Star," say a prayer that sounds like a menu order, gaze at the dark moon's light, and drift off to sleep dreaming about her Knight in Shining Armor.

Every dream features scene after scene of being pampered, showered with love, lots of attention, gifts, defended, and spoiled; smiles and laughter; hugs and kisses; long, flowing hair blowing in the breeze of a cool summer's eve; and white, billowy chiffon billowing all over the place because that trusty steed is moving like a rocket-- but neither she nor her knight goes tumbling off onto the ground. Her dreams defy gravity and reality.

The little girl and her knight are secure and deliriously happy forever and ever. That's the plan. That's the dream, and no little girl is settling for less, until, of course, the only trace of her lives deep inside the heart of the grown woman she becomes. The grown woman wants to be free of that naïve little girl and her wishful thinking, but they are forever joined to each other. Year after year the dream fails to come true. The little girl continues to hope. Every now and then, when the grown woman is not careful, the little girl escapes and reveals herself through tears, words, and actions. Whatever she became when she grew up, no matter how praiseworthy or impressive; never eclipses what she always wanted to be protected, cared for —loved.

2

FOUNDATION

While in grade school, I recall a teacher asking my classmates and I, "What do you *want* to be when you grow up?" Some said they wanted to become doctors or lawyers, while others dreamed of being teachers, fire- fighters, or police officers. I think most of the girls in my class all aspired to be something greater, but the thought of marrying a doctor, lawyer, teacher, firefighter, or a police officer seemed as equally appealing as becoming one.

The teacher didn't ask what we *dreamed* to be. Would our answers have been different or less ordinary? As a young girl, I believed that my dream would come true. To have a great career and marry someone whose career was equally great or greater didn't seem unreasonable or impossible. That was my dream-to have it all: a great career, doting husband that provides and a loving family.

Growing up in a military family, I watched my father, an Army officer, exude strength and perseverance. My mother matched his attributes, and appearances mattered greatly to her. We had to look our best, and she really didn't spare any cost to make sure that we did. Frivolous things weren't important to my dad. Actually, he wasn't impressed with material things at all. Needs mattered. Paying bills on time, being financially responsible, and having the basics were all that counted as far as dad was concerned. The differences in my parents' view of what was, and was not, important were the source of growing friction. One wanted everything, and the other could be quite content with so much less.

My experience with my dad would color my expectations in my future relationships with men. My dad was hardworking and dependable. He was also consistent. His "yes" wasn't a "maybe" and his "no" was definite. With him, you knew exactly what you were getting. He was honest - not brutally, but he meant what he said. There were no words between the lines that contradicted what was in the lines. He was a strong, hard working and I loved him. I never wondered whether or not he loved or wanted, my four sisters and me. I knew it. I could see it and feel it. Children do know, and he always reassured us. We felt safe. I dreamed of having a man like that in my life. It never occurred to me to see him through my mother's eyes. Was she happy?

No. They divorced. Tumultuous relationship. My mother forgave my dad. She taught us to forgive also, no matter what was done to us. She also taught us to forget.

3

STARRY EYES

In high school, I thought that I was far more mature than other girls my age. I always felt as if I was *too* mature. I felt as if I'd grown up before my time. Perhaps I was suppressing something I didn't yet understand.

I was very interested in school. I was a networking machine before there was a word for "networking." Building relationships mattered. I thought that was the key to being successful. I met all types of people and learned as much as I could from them. With each experience, I was sure that my perspectives concerning life were evolving! You couldn't tell me that I was not an independent woman! There I was, a high school senior, and I thought I had the master keys to life. I was upwardly mobile, headed for the world of advanced studies, work, and career success. Then, I, the budding "Every Woman" fell in love with my neighbor. All of the networking, moving and shaking had been a place holder. What I really longed for was companionship and love.

The notion that someone adored me and wanted to be in my company was explosive. That explosion woke up the dreaming little girl inside. Her knight had arrived. Sir Loving, my special friend, was everything, well, *almost* everything she hoped he would be. He swept her off her feet—and joined her in bed, except there was more than sleeping and dreaming taking place.

4

OPEN EYES

I was 17 and pregnant. The frantic ringing of wedding bells seized priority and drowned out the ringing of school bells. It's funny how we insist on doing "the right thing" *after* we've done the wrong thing.

The dreamy-eyed little girl was beside herself with glee. There would be a *real* baby doll to love, and her knight would care for them both. "Happily ever after" was so close she could touch it, and she twirled until she'd made herself dizzy. Suddenly, another, new, unfamiliar, somber voice began speaking, one that interrupted her celebrating. "You've made a mistake—a big mistake. *Don't* have a baby at your age! Don't *marry* that little boy! You are *much* too young! You need to explore all of life's opportunities first! You need to go to *school*! You have *too* much to offer."

I didn't know if it was the voice of intuition, nerves, or the overflow of my gut as my belly continued to swell. I wondered if it was God trying to get my attention.

I know *now* that if we just stop, sit quietly, and incline our ears to hear, we'll realize that God *is* speaking to us. He has something to say *all* of the time—not just in the midst of a Sunday morning service. Filling our lives with busy-ness and noise causes us to miss very clear warnings and specific directions that impact our tomorrows. All I could see and hear were the romantic sounds of what was happening right then. I was in love. The only *future* events on which I could concentrate were a visit to the Justice of the Peace, and a stay in a hospital maternity ward. I was having a wedding. I would be a bride. I would be a mother. I would be a wife. Whether it was the dream version or not didn't matter—even though it should have.

My knight *had* no shining armor, trusty steed, sword, wealth, power, or kingdom. He *had* no responsibilities other than doing his homework, cutting grass, and cleaning up his room. Someone else was providing and caring for *him*. How could *he* adequately care for *me?* Some things were too overwhelming to consider. It meant listening to and heeding the words of the somber voice that seemed to be in favor of me being alone. It seemed insensitive.

The little girl continued to celebrate. "Something old, something new, something borrowed, something blue!" She was becoming annoying, but she was right. Tradition was important! I *had* to collect those things or it certainly wouldn't be a real wedding, would it?

The once non-negotiable criteria concerning my future suddenly became flexible. The promise of a bright and prosperous future with the man of my dreams wasn't supposed to inspire skepticism or fear.

Looking back, I really can't be sure if he was Sir Loving, the knight of my dreams, an angel in disguise who was strangely helping me to *fulfill* my dreams, or the ordinary guy who would challenge me to *wake the heck up*.

My dream of being married was not as much about the man as it was about the dream itself. I wanted what I thought my mother had. Love and security. What I dreamed she had.

5

WEARY EYES

I gave birth to a beautiful, healthy baby boy. What started out as a great idea and seemed like a heavenly match, turned out to be a grossly premature decision fueled by fiction and overactive hormones. I was miserable. The moral of the lovesick story of a little girl longing to spread her wings and fly was, "Stay in the safety and security of the nest as long as you can."

The expectation and hope that my son inspired was not enough to sustain my marriage. A part of me knew that the fairy tale had ended long before we'd been pronounced husband and wife. After five years of enduring the incessant, vicious meddling of family members, and my husband's drug use, I decided that my son and I had a much better chance on our own.

It is shocking how quickly sentiments change. Perhaps out of frustration, or immaturity, my young husband began to blame me for all that was wrong in his life. Strangely, his father did, too. The cruel, disparaging words his father spoke clearly disregarded that I had given birth to his first grandchild. My once gallant Sir Charming slowly morphed into a pitiful Sir Cowardly. He just stood silently by as his father berated me, "You *need* us! What are you going to do without my family's support? You ain't gonna amount to *nothing*!"

The little girl inside didn't understand. "Me? Nothing? *Me?*" His words bruised her. Whoever created the "Sticks and Stones" ditty must have had the thickest skin in the universe. He'd said "Nothing." No prospect of advancement or satisfaction. No apparent value. I would be nonexistent. No significance. *Me?* Nothing? Something stirred inside me when I considered his words -- something that immediately stopped my tears. I may have been his daughter-in-law briefly enough for him to think that I no longer had an identity, but I knew that I was *still* my tenacious father's daughter; my proud mother's reflection; the apple of God's eye. I had worth. I'd always been told that I was valuable. His words, so vastly different than the loving ones I was accustomed to hearing, were motivation in disguise. The problem was that I was so motivated to prove him wrong, that I didn't consider that it wasn't necessary for me to prove *anything* to him at all. It had never been my assignment. I'd just given that task to myself, and in doing so, I gave him more power and credibility than he deserved.

But at the same time, it empowered me to strive to be somebody in life.

6

LESSONS

After my marriage ended, I realized that there was much more to being a wife than romance novels and movies bothered to reveal. I learned that marriage was not only an act of love but also an act of faith. I was too young and immature to understand any of that but it didn't stop me from trying.

When the music stops, and after the wedding bells have rung for the final time, there's *real* life to live, and I was not prepared for it. The changes were startling. The notion that family members could be envious of my child, who was such an integral part of me, was difficult to understand. I thought I knew what was important in life. I thought I had enough experience from which to draw from. I had nothing to rely on. I had to realize that I was not my mother, and my husband was not my father. My parents' marriage was *not* mine. I had been playing house based on a very good script, and mental notes that I thought I'd memorized. I couldn't take chapters from *their* pages and infuse them into *our* book or to rewrite their pages the way they should have been.. That would not be reasonable. I couldn't change my husband, his views, habits, actions, or his family. I couldn't will him to be ready for the responsibilities of a family. I was more than equipped to handle how things were *supposed* to be. How things actually *were* was too much for both of us.

I realized that finding a genuine knight/soldier, who had the backbone and tenacity of my father and was the brave horseman of my childhood dreams, would be a bit challenging. I was wondering if my mother's good fortune, where a man was concerned, would ever visit me. To me, she had it made, but I had never asked her if *she* felt fortunate. I'd always placed my father on a pedestal. Because *he* was perfect, every other man should have been as well. He was the standard. He was MY standard. But, that's how the little girl in me is. She see's what she wants to see. Daddy was not a hero.

I'd approached marriage wearing huge, rose-colored glasses that altered my 20/20 vision drastically. The twinkle, twinkle in the little star seemed to have a short in its fuse, the Wonderland was a façade that could have been broken down and hauled away in a truck, and my street didn't seem to have a permit for trusty steed traffic. It was neither wide nor smooth enough. My fairy tale was dissipating with a baby in tow.

Focusing on work distracted me from my bruised dreams. It was, of course the *adult* thing to do. I told myself that there were other ways to "do" life. Everyone didn't have to be married. I decided to shelve the "knight in shining armor" quest for a while. I told myself to forget the brave soldier and concentrate on building a successful career. I wasn't settling. I figured if I immersed myself in work, I wouldn't have time to lament not having someone with whom to share the results of a blissful, happy life. I was still busy trying to prove I was "somebody."

7

DENIAL

All of my new declarations and affirmations sounded good for a while. So often, I just wanted to make myself feel better. Two years after my first marriage ended; however, I was in love again. I was so attracted to Sir Charming when he dashed onto the scene, that I *ended* a decent relationship. (Oh yes, there was always someone in the wings.) I cringe when I think of my reasons, but the respectful boyfriend I promptly kicked to the curb was a bit nerdy and the relationship was mov- ing too slowly. Apparently, I had not learned anything about moving too *quickly*.

My new obsession was flirty, cocky, strong, handsome, and always made me smile and even giggle. I was so focused on his potential and was eager to date him. Plus, I was getting restless and slightly bored from dating the "decent" guy. This time, I would be ready, I said to myself. I thought I'd asked myself all of the right questions before going down that path again:

> Can you survive another heartbreak?
> How will a second trip to the altar turn out?
> Will it work this time?
> Will you be happy?
> Will he make a great step-father?
> Will he be a genuine partner?

THE LITTLE GIRL INSIDE

How long before his good looks fade?
Is his charm real or fake?

Even as I approached the actual altar, I considered that I could be making yet another huge mistake. I wasn't sure if I was a dress-up bride or a dressed-up fool-- or both! It wasn't a long walk, but I'm sure I second guessed myself a thousand times between the entrance to the chapel and the altar. I had invited my family, all of my closest friends, supervisors, and coworkers. The chapel was filled, and Father Samuel was going to make it all official. My mind was all over the place. Where was the secret trap door for me to disappear into? It would be too embarrassing to tell everyone I had suddenly changed my mind. What about all of those nice gifts people had taken their time to choose for us? I couldn't crack all of those smiling faces, and they were genuinely smiling just for me. At my right and my left there were people cheesing. Why wouldn't one of them have a nervous breakdown or pass out, or go into labor, or start a fire? Maybe one of them would yell out a list of reasons when Father Samuel asked if there was anyone who knew of a reason why we shouldn't be joined together. Maybe I would just snap, or yell out, or faint myself.

My dad didn't give me away. That should have been a sign. His back problems should have been a sign! Didn't I hear the voices in my head? "This isn't strong! This isn't stable! Bail out! Bail OUT!" My Uncle Billy stood in for my dad. He was so proud to do it. He should have tripped me. I *knew* I was making a mistake. Sir Charming had two sons from a previous relationship and hadn't ever chosen to marry their mother. That should have sent me bolting for the nearest door. Once again, I felt I could make it all better. I thought I had enough love for everyone.

I was moving in slow motion in my new cream lace dress. The little girl wanted a white dress so badly. She thought it would cancel out the memory of my first mistake. For her, every new picture deserved a flawless, clean sheet of paper.

As I walked, I stared into everyone's miserably happy faces. They were thinking I'd struck gold, and there I was thinking I needed and deserved more than the committed phobic playboy I was facing. The *first* time I'd considered matrimony, I wanted a wedding. This time I wanted a *marriage*. Both times I had major doubts about longevity. Sir Charming was watching me head towards him, and I'm sure we were thinking the same thing. "What the heck am I doing?!" I managed to silence the voices in my head, and he must have done the same, because we both said, "I do."

For the second time, I was married and in love, and praying that it was the last time. I gave birth to two beautiful daughters. The fifteen years of marriage proved to be more exhausting than the labor I endured to deliver them. To rehash the details of troubled years would drain energy as well. Some things you just want to forget or, wait for the "whole story."

8

LOST

I decided it was time for me to put my aspiration to be a wife on a very high shelf--one that I would need a rope and a ladder to reach. I felt I had failed as a woman, wife and a mother. If my mother's example was any indication, and the rules in my fairy tale manual were accurate, keeping one's family intact was a major skill and characteristic of a real woman.

Once again, I turned my attention to motherhood and career. I wanted to be a good example for my children. I wanted them to be proud of me. What they thought of me mattered terribly. Two failed marriages threatened to color my opinion of myself, but I fought the inclination to use myself as a punching bag. I focused on my childrens futures, and I needed to be alert and functioning to do that. They had to be academically strong.

They were going to be college graduates. They would be able to take care of themselves. I wanted them to make good choices that didn't derail their lives, or cause them pain, shame, or even loss.

As independent and strong as I believed I'd become, love and companionship were always on my mind. I did *not* want to be alone. I always thought that a man completed "the family." It didn't seem normal or natural being a single parent. I was *supposed* to "have the man." It closed the circle. I wasn't supposed to be doing life by myself.

There were roles to which I wasn't supposed to be assigned. It hadn't been my experience. Women did *this*. Men did *that*. All I felt in my heart was the rhythm of the words "mommy, daddy and children." They belonged together.

    I was still hopeful that I was capable of loving someone and worthy of being loved. I had more to offer, I reasoned. I was wiser, and financially stable. Surely I was a good catch. Maybe if I just started falling, someone would catch me.

9

FAST FORWARD

I couldn't believe my son was about to enter college. Time seemed to speed by so quickly. He was doing his part to get into college, while I, too, was working toward my degree. I wanted to be a good example. Part of proving that I was "something" was for each of my children to be successful. I couldn't fail motherhood, and I was determined that they *would* not fail. It was important for them to know that education was critical to their success.

Spending time with my children was like medicine. I wanted them to know they could always depend on me, talk to me, come to me with any problem, share their thoughts, dreams, and goals. I wasn't attempting to be a friend, I was their mother; but how they perceived me boosted how I perceived myself. Failing them wasn't an option. My confidence as a woman had suffered, but motherhood would not ever be a weak point.

For years, I'd positioned myself to be promoted on the job. I eagerly took on new assignments and responsibilities. Stress at my office was always present, but every challenge seemed to project the faces of my children. I'd tell myself, "You're doing this for them. You can do it. Finish the task."

My needs took a bit of a back seat. Maybe I didn't need to be a part of a couple. Maybe I *could* manage alone. I was *doing* it, wasn't I? Did I really want to complicate my life? There were three people who were depending on me. They deserved my undivided attention. I could be all things to them—mom, chauffeur, cook, laundress, tutor, nurse, mediator, bank, barber, beautician, stylist, recreation coordinator, spiritual advisor, and giver of great hugs. They, however, could not be all things to me, and it would be neither fair nor sensible to expect them to be. My son wasn't the little man of the house, he was my *son*. My daughters weren't girlfriends I could dish the dirt with. They needed a *mother*. Children have a right to just be children. I couldn't visit my issues upon them.

There's nothing like busyness and even crowds to expose how alone you feel at times. I had to learn how to be genuinely content and enjoy my own company.

I thought I had my stuff together. I tried to tell myself so. Perhaps my desire to be loved was sending signals into the atmosphere of which I wasn't aware.

10

A BLAST FROM MY PAST

The little girl in me was celebrating again. My first sweetheart from elementary school appeared out of nowhere. He was living in Seattle, so we chatted for months before we eventually met face to face.

I had to attend a conference in San Francisco and we met in the hotel lobby. He brought back so many good memories of my childhood and summers spent in South Carolina. He brought a smile to my face just like he'd always done when I was a child.

I found out that he'd recently divorced and had a son and a daughter. Before I knew it, we started dating. We agreed to meet whenever time permitted, and it wasn't long before Cupid's arrows knocked both of us out cold.

We were children when we met, and we giddily picked up right where we left off, except we were taller, parents, and divorcees. Within a year, he proposed, went to a jewelry store, and confirmed his intentions by giving me a 2.5 carat diamond ring.

"Yes" fell out of my mouth before I even considered that we lived in two different states across the country. Being happy overshadowed the need to ask all of the obvious, pertinent questions. What about our living arrangements? Who would relocate where? What about our children? How were the relationships with our respective former spouses? Will our families get along?

We were like kids on a playground all over again. We'd been wounded, and now, it seemed that the innocence of childhood had erased all of our pain. Surely it was fate. The pertinent questions would have to wait. Love would take care of the messy details. Didn't it always?

Within three months of joining in holy matrimony at our lavish wedding, attended by both of our families, a celebration that decreased our bank accounts by $30,000, we separated. Within twelve months we were legally divorced.

He'd never stopped loving his wife. The idea that she was jealous of his new bride was all the information he needed to pack his things and head back home to Seattle. He still loved her. I was devastated. But not so devastated that I didn't send him back home the moment he revealed he still loved her and missed her terribly.

We never saw one another again. The little girl in me had lost her playmate. I'd served my purpose. I'd been used to make her jealous and it worked. Why hadn't I been good enough? Why wasn't I the chosen one? His actions hurt more than I cared to admit. I could now boast three failed marriages. I had to fight the inclination to deem myself a failure. There were times, however, when that was exactly the way I felt.

11

A BREATH OF FRESH AIR

Maybe I should have stayed indoors for a while and hybernated. Surely the words "desperate," "lonely," and "needy" weren't radiating from my being like neon, were they?

Could I have been advertising for someone to comfort me? What was I subconsciously or deliberately drawing to myself? Was it my voice, my walk or my countenance that screamed, "Yes, I need you!"

My third marriage was over. I'd been blindsided. I was so hurt that I became self-conscious. It was as if there was a cartoon balloon over my head that read, "She's been married three times. Stay away from her..."

I wasn't looking for love, like, or fun when I ran into a man who seemed to be "a breath of fresh air." He was a policeman, a bit mysterious, suave, and quite attractive. The uniform was a bit of a turn-on, too. Of course although I told myself to take it slowly, just the sight of him prompted me to move expeditiously. We began dating.

Our relationship was much more casual than the others had been. I reasoned that it was exactly what I needed at the time. "No serious commitment, no emotional attachment," I told myself. "Just have a good time and enjoy the man's company. There's no harm in that."

I *did* enjoy his company—very much—until I received a phone call from someone who *also* enjoyed his company...and his bed... and his life...regularly...intimately...*and* she had her own set of keys.

Officer Wrong had a live-in girlfriend. Her preferred title, of course, was fiancé.

It's interesting how people neglect to share critical pieces of information that might impact your decision to give them a second look, let alone your phone number. How does one forget a detail like a housemate? She, however, had no intention to remain a secret. I can't say I blamed her.

I didn't have tears or time to waste. That chapter opened and closed so fast it was almost comical, but I still had to consider how easily I had been drawn into his world. There were obvious signs. Why hadn't I seen them? Why didn't I heed them? Why didn't I ask more questions? Why didn't I know? Did I want to know?

12

LOVE AND TECHNOLOGY

For two years, I was a bit numb. Church, family, edu-cation, and career were all that my life's list had room for.

Church was just what I needed. I'm wasn't sure, at the time, how much I was actually learning, or if I was just mesmerized by the music, and high pitched reminders of what God was "getting ready to do," in my life. As if the preacher was talking directly to me in spite of the fact there were hundreds in the congregation. How much money I gave apparently determined how quickly I would see results in my life. Hope would begin to fade as soon as I exited the church parking lot. For a few hours, though, I *felt* better. Yet, deep down inside, I knew God was with me in the pits of my stomach. I felt His presence.

My friend Naomi thought I should permanently bury thoughts of Sir Knight, Sir Charming, the Playmate, and Officer Wrong, and squeeze Internet dating onto my list of things to do. I thought she was nuts and I told her so. I'd seen the news, not interested. I'd invited many things into my life, but a serial killer hadn't been one of them. I just couldn't wrap my mind around meeting someone via the Internet. Meeting people the old fashioned way hadn't exactly helped me to hit the relationship jackpot, but "face to face" was the route I intended to take if I ever decided to take my heart out of moth balls again.

Naomi was having a great time meeting people with whom she had chatted online, but it seemed risky and scary to me. I told her that if she ever again decided to go on a date with someone she'd met online, that she shouldn't do it alone. I told her I'd go with her, not knowing she'd accept another invitation so quickly. I reluctantly agreed to join her for dinner at a local restaurant so that she could become better acquainted with her Internet suitor.

After a long work week, the last thing I wanted to do was sit across a table making small talk with strangers. I began to regret telling Naomi that I'd join her that night. Meeting guys online was not my thing, didn't I tell her that? I hadn't been out socially in a long time, though, and decided that my attitude needed a little adjusting. Maybe it wouldn't be so bad. Besides, I was starving, and how would I feel if I turned on the news the next day and Naomi's body was being fished out of the river or something? As exhausted as I was, I had to support my girl. It was apparent by her complimentary words that she was seriously interested in the guy. Somebody had to be happy in my world, and I admit I was a bit curious and excited for her.

As I approached the restaurant, I was hoping that Naomi's experience would go well. Part of me wanted to speed out of the parking lot, get home to my daughters and watch a Lifetime movie, but I saw Naomi's SUV.

When we got to the restaurant, Naomi scanned the room for her date. All she had to go by was a blurry photograph. Two guys were sitting at tables near the enormous bar. It was a sports lover's venue. I is or was a girly girl. The room was crowded and noisy. That Lifetime movie was calling my name. What was I *doing* there? Why hadn't I gone home where I *belonged*?

Neither man stood up to greet us as we approached them. It was funny how I always imposed my codes of behavior on everyone. I was well versed in what was polite, what was proper, and what ought and ought *not to* happen. Home training dictated what they *should* have done. Lack of familiarity and freewill dictated what they *did*. I had to remember that everyone was not raised in my parent's home. Everyone was not raised to know proper etiquette.

They introduced themselves--Jamar and Gaines-- and motioned for us to sit down. Perhaps the laid back environment was to blame for their lack of chivalry. Perhaps they had photographs, too, and didn't know who or what to expect. After getting past the less than warm welcome, Jamar's strikingly handsome smile, slim build, and tall frame let me know that, at least superficially, Naomi had chosen well. I was a bit ashamed of myself for looking at him so intently. The Lord had definitely spent quality time fashioning his exterior. He was tall and handsome!

Gaines, on the other hand, looked more like a fisherman taking a break for a smoke. It was clear that he didn't have membership at a gym or even the directions *to* one. The dull green jacket he wore didn't do too much for him. He had an olive complexion and was pleasant enough, but not exactly my type. Why had I even considered whether he was my type at all? I had to remind myself of my track record with "my type" and remember I wasn't there to date, or get married, just to enjoy a meal and support a friend.

Jamar seemed to be disinterested in Naomi. I could not help but notice how dismissive he was. His abrupt, one-word answers screamed, "I don't want to be bothered." Gaines picked up on my irritation and tried to distract me from their conversation by creating small talk of his own. I was just as dismissive of Gaines as Jamar was of Naomi. The conversation was going nowhere. Didn't he know what an awesome woman my friend was? What was wrong with him? The more she tried to pull responses from him, the more agitated I became. Meanwhile, Gaines was doing everything in his power to divert my attention from their conversation. He began asking me questions. I finally decided to engage Gaines--hoping to distract myself from desperately wanting to punch Jamar in the face for being so rude to my friend.

I opened up to Gaines about my divorce, children, and talked a little about my family. I wasn't holding back any details and wasn't sure why. Had it been so long since I actually talked to someone? Did I *need* to talk? Lord knows I was doing a *lot* of it. He seemed especially intrigued by the fact that my late father had been an Army officer. He, too, had been an officer. After answering all of his questions, I let him know that I was aware that he was trying to keep me from my "wingman" duties, but that didn't stop him from coming up with a new round of questions. The more Gaines and I talked, the more interesting the conversation became. The more he mentioned where he lived, what he owned and drove, the more his attire and appearance didn't seem to be such a turn off. It should have been a warning of what was wrong in my own heart. The words "gated community" seemed to make him considerably more attractive.

I soon forgot all about Naomi and Jamar. "She's an adult," I thought, and I needed to lighten up. Perhaps I was projecting my own fears onto her. If she wasn't bothered, why was I?

Gaines's conversation was quite enjoyable. He talked about his twin brother, his military career, his grown daughter and her wedding, his parents, his Georgia roots, his home near the ninth hole of a golf course, and his rather large dog who probably was due for a walk and wondering where his owner was.

I glanced over to see if Naomi's evening was meeting my expectations, and wanted her to be a part of our conversation instead. A little over an hour had passed and no one had mentioned food. I'd had my share of beverages though, and excused myself to go to the ladies room. Maybe it was a bit vain on my part, but in my black sweater dress, I did wonder whose eyes were watching me as I walked away. Gaines asked for my phone number when I got back to the table. I gave him a handwritten note with my work and cell number. He gave me someone else's business card and wrote a number he instructed me to use as his work, home and business contact. Gaines paid the bill for the drinks, but Naomi and I didn't eat anything, nor did the guys offer.

As we left the restaurant, Jamar walked along with Gaines, and Naomi and I exited the restaurant together. Gaines walked us both to our cars as Jamar scurried to his own car alone, without looking back or even waving "good night." An evening that began as a support mission ended with me wondering if I wasn't done with relationships after all.

13

AGAIN

A serious relationship may have been the *last* thing on my mind, but obviously it was *on* my mind just the same. What started out as just a night out with a stranger quickly followed the same pattern as my previous rela- tionships. I did not know Gaines very well. I didn't know him at all, but something seemed familiar. After a history of bad endings, I should have been a lot more cautious and a little less trusting, but I wasn't. I liked the feeling—the *idea* of a relationship. Gaines was so unassuming, subtle, and very intelligent. His conversation was different. I began to trust him. I presumed that this eccentric man didn't have the wherewithal to be cruel. I recall thinking, "Oh, God I don't need any more heartaches. Let him be who he says he is. Let me be safe with him." Instead of wishing and praying, I should have just taken advantage of technology and answered my own questions.

I had so many unresolved issues, unmet needs and unhealed wounds. I had to be careful about making hasty decisions. My heart may as well have been held together by string and duct tape, and I hadn't been guarding it well at all. Gaines was assuring me that he wasn't going to damage my heart any further. Gaines quickly became Sir Intellectual in my life.

Sir Intellectual was quickly exceeding the imaginary limit of how many phone calls in a single day are too many. If we were not together, he was on the other end of the line or leaving a message. He paid more attention to me than anyone ever had. He had an endless library of stories and I listened to every one of them. He tearfully told me about the helicopter accident that killed his wife who had been a military medic. Her body had never been recovered. I felt so much compassion for him. I knew the relief of seeing a loved one return home from being deployed. To have no closure at all was something I couldn't imagine. I mourned for her. She was a mother like me. I ached for him. There had been no bitterness or trouble between them, and suddenly she was gone. He'd left West Point abruptly before graduating and rushed home to marry her. He had accepted her son as his own and gladly given him his name. They'd welcomed a baby girl and watched her grow. There was love between them. It didn't seem fair for things to end so tragically.

He raised both children with the help of their families. Both children seemed to have adjusted well, and he continued to look after them during their adult years, even though he'd relocated to Maryland for work and they were in Michigan.

The more he shared, the more I admired and respected him. If Sir Intellectual wasn't telling me how awful it was to lose his wife, he was telling me how brave and dedicated she was, and how much she loved him. He was suffering still, and the nurturer in me was ready to come to the rescue. I simply didn't know what to say, but I was determined to be there.

In the wake of her death, Sir Intellectual told me that he stood to receive a sizable settlement. In the meantime, he struggled to pay his bills. As he waited on his wife's estate to be settled, there were many challenges in keeping his home. He just wanted out and wanted to downsize. He'd decided on a condominium in Washington, D.C. I had been dating him for eight weeks and had seen *neither* home.

I often asked him if I could help him unpack. He would say that he was a neat person and would be embarrassed if I saw all the mess in his new condo. He wanted my first impression to be a great one. While he was determined not to allow me to come to his home until he was pleased with the environment, I was beginning to wonder if he was keeping something from me. He said he would have to make the time to decipher what he would keep in the condo and what to place in storage. I felt so helpless, not being able to assist him. I never heard anything else about the home in the gated community, only that he was living amongst boxes in a messy condo.

Sir Intellectual seemed overwhelmed and I was trying to help as best I could without completely interfering in his affairs. I could not imagine having to manage an estate, maintain a distant relationship with two grown children and their grandparents, and plan for early retirement. He spoke of devoting time to writing poetry, which endeared me to him even more.

On his last day at his office, he was favored with a party. When I asked if any of his family came to support him, he insisted that having his coworkers in attendance was more than enough for him. He'd never been in favor of mixing business and family. I thought that something as significant as retirement called for an exception to the business/pleasure rule. Shouldn't everyone who was meaningful in your life be there to celebrate with you? Then it hit me. We were dating and I hadn't been invited *either*. Maybe he was embarrassed that he was ten years older than me.

The time we spent together increased after his retirement. I learned just how talented and versatile he was. In addition to being a writer, he was also a musician and quite a good cook. I thought he was content with retirement and was surprised when he accepted a new job. At odd hours, he would often get calls from work. The person on the line was always demanding and impatient. Sir Intellectual's schedule was irregular and he'd often set his own hours. There was always urgency about the job and I often found myself feeling suspicious. I could hardly understand any of the conversations because they were either loaded with technical terms or heated words. He would often excuse himself and finish calls in another room or outside. He just seemed to have so much information in his head and no one seemed to be able to manage without him. I thought he was brilliant. I also thought it was past time that he and my family meet.

My eldest daughter thought he was nerdy and not nearly as fun to be around as her father. I wasn't surprised that she would make a comparison. My youngest daughter liked him because he always took her side if there was a difference of opinion. She needed to be supported. My son thought he was a bit weird, but really didn't care one way or another. I wonder if he shook his head and thought, "Here she goes again". My mother heard the words "retired Army colonel" and immediately thought "benefits," "commissary," and "good catch." He mentioned his football playing family member and she thought, "free seats." She'd learned the importance of security. Love was good, but food, clothing and shelter were better.

I thought it was time to introduce him to my coworkers. I admit I had someone conduct a background check, but the results didn't provide me with the details I wanted. His records were sealed. "Who was this man?" That was a question I'd neglected to ask. Had he been conducting secret level assignments? Was he a spy? Was he a private investigator? Was he even a human being? Was he a super hero? The little girl in me was celebrating again. We were celebrating because I was dating someone special, brilliant, powerful, mysterious, and important! My daddy would be so proud of me, I thought.

I could not stop talking about him to everyone I met, especially my coworkers. I mentioned his name to my supervisor. He asked me several times to repeat his name. He would always give me a strange, blue-eyed stare, as if he wanted to share incriminating information but wanted me to discover it first. I ignored it, remained gleeful.

Sir Intellectual and I continued dating. I was "wifey" material, he'd say. He appreciated how I listened to story after story, and I hung on every word as he spoke. He seemed to have connections everywhere. There was always a friend who could hook him up with this or that. He would give my son and nephews complimentary tickets to football games. He told me his nephew played for the team so getting ticket with good seats was easy for him. That made the kids very happy. Gifts tend to cause young people to warm up to a person. And, making my family happy made me happy.

He helped me organize my bills on a spreadsheet As much as I tried to stay on top of things, I was always disorganized in this area and needed lots of improvement. He was so good in finances. He even started coming over after work to cook for us. Before I knew it, I became a stranger in my own kitchen. He was a constant presence, and began using a phrase I'd never heard before: "dating exclusively." Why didn't I realize that it implied he had never stopped casually dating *other* women?

When he asked me to marry him, I reasoned that I didn't have any other suitors. I had often said I wanted a Christian man to help me raise my children. He certainly seemed to qualify. He quoted scriptures a lot, but with my limited knowledge, he could have been quoting "Poor Richard's Almanac." I concluded that God had sent him as a consolation prize for the disastrous relationships of my past. Maybe God was finally getting around to doing what all of the preachers said he would do. Once again, I said, "Yes" to a proposal. I dusted off the old list I'd created in my head:

1. Godly
2. Family man
3. Integrity
4. Intelligent
5. Businessman
6. Trustworthy
7. Hero
8. Affectionate
9. Protective
10. Love, Love, Love and Love

What else did I need? Sir Intellectual proposed and gave me a beautiful, princess cut, two-carat diamond ring. My attention to *those* kinds of details, and not the truly important ones, would get me into trouble time and time again.

I don't recall how he proposed. Maybe I was blinded by the bling. I just remember him placing the ring on my finger, and it sent me into immediate planning mode. I had to tell the children and my mother, who would *all* remind me that this would be marriage number *four*. Counseling had to precede finding a dress or shoes. I needed a different foundation on which to build this time, but wondered if I was building the same old house.

Maybe I should have enlisted the services of a stranger, someone who could be objective, but I sought the advice of a female minister who knew about my failed marriages and yet she never judged or criticized me—at least not to my face. She explained to me that counseling would last about six weeks. Could everything I hadn't learned before be squeezed into such a short span of time? Would I emerge an expert on how to sustain a marriage and finally achieve "ever after" happiness? Gaines agreed to counseling and I braced myself to tell my family that they would be invited to yet another wedding.

14

AND AGAIN

When I announced to my family that I was marrying again, they showed no emotion. They looked at each other, then looked at me. It was as if words were trying to form, but the words got stuck in all of their throats.

It's funny how much importance many women place on their ability to "get a man." I'd gotten one, once again, and they were supposed to be impressed, or envious, or happy or *something*. Why weren't they happy for me? I wanted them to say "Congratulations" or show *some* signs of approval, but they just stared blankly.

I should have expected their silence, and considered that silence *is* a response. Embarrassment rose up inside me. It should have been a warning. My own emotions were trying to get my attention, but that darned little girl inside me was jumping up and down. She was going to be a pretty princess again. They didn't have to be happy. She was.

I didn't want my friends and coworkers to tease or dissuade me, so I kept my plans from everyone but my three closest friends. Why hadn't they wrestled me to the ground and demanded I think it over? I suppose people root for love all the time. They didn't want to monsoon all over my newest parade. Maybe everyone was saying to themselves, "it could stick this time."

I told everyone they could forgo looking for anything special to wear, as if I was doing them a favor. Who said they'd even thought about it? What would they be celebrating—me or my lack of good judgment? I just wanted them to be there— and be happy for me. Lasting happiness was on the way. The little girl in me was delirious again. She just leapt, as always, without looking first to see if there was a net, water in the pool, or a working parachute to strap on. Happiness was all she'd ever really wanted. She was insulated inside me. If I hit the ground as I'd done many times before, she'd only experience the adventure, not the pain.

Our counselor should have spent a *lot* more time with me. She should have risked the possibility of me getting defensive or angry and told me the bitter truth. She should have abandoned correctness and tact. Sure, God is forgiving, and bans fishing in the "Sea of Forgetfulness," but he also encourages the attainment of wisdom. She should have fished up everything I was trying to forget and held it up for me to see. She should have demanded that I slow down. Instead, our counselor stuck to the script—a script that would have been applicable for a couple whose faith was established and strong. It would even have been ideal for someone who was marrying for the first time. Perhaps in not wanting to hurt my feelings, she glossed over the realities of my life; skipped over sensitive subjects, disregarded her own discernment, and ignored the fact that I should have avoided another marriage like grim death. Maybe she was brimming with hope and in love with love, like me. Maybe she knew I was going to do what I wanted to in spite of her recommendations. I know that she meant well. She too wanted me to be happy.

She began by telling us that it was important to start a marriage on a solid foundation. According to her philosophy, the first appropriate thing to do was to thank the people who brought us into the world. She said we should give credit to them, and express our gratitude in writing. I had never honored my parents in such a manner--nor had Sir Intellectual. I don't know why, but neither of us ever got around to writing those letters. Maybe there were things we didn't think our parents deserved credit for; areas where we felt they had actually failed us, but never had the courage to articulate.

We were instructed to meet with all of our children and share our plans, agree to tithe regularly, save for our children's college educations, open joint savings accounts, secure life and health insurance coverage, and write wills. We were also instructed to fast from 6 a.m. to 6 p.m. Finally, we were given specific passages of scripture to study: Deuteronomy 28:1-15, 1 Chronicles 4:10, Matthew 18:18, Titus 2:3, Titus 2:13-14 and Psalm 91. She told us to never lose sight that God is above all.

I read the material and studied it, and stored it away. I hadn't hearkened "diligently to the voice" of anyone except that little girl inside my head who wanted to be a bride. Yeah. *Sure.* God may have given me power to tread over serpents, but he didn't tell me to go *looking* for them to prove how thoroughly I could do it. I wanted blessings, but blessings had conditions, and I hadn't honored my part of the bargain. I was eager to do only one thing—get married, and dwell with, be covered by, and take refuge in my husband.

It would be a while before I acknowledged God's name and realized he was the only one who could truly rescue me.

We met with our counselor twice a week prior to the wedding. Each time we met, she asked us what we liked about each other. Each time she asked Sir Intellectual, he never looked directly at her, but he always said something about my kindness. I shared how I enjoyed his company, his patience with my girls, and the example he set for my son even though he was no longer at home. My answers were always deliberate and detailed. He, on the other hand, always seemed to be fishing for something to say. I took it to be he may be somewhat shy.

As the wedding date neared, I noticed that every dress in my closet was a little tight. I had been a perfect size 12 for years and nothing I tried on seemed to fit. Why hadn't I noticed that it had been six weeks since my last period? I hurried to a nearby pharmacy to purchase a pregnancy test. I hadn't slept with anyone except Sir Intellectual and he'd undergone a vasectomy, but I was anxious about the results. I had reason to be. I was pregnant!

Had I misunderstood him? Had he said *appendectomy*? I asked him about it, and he told me that occasionally the procedures don't work. I guess he was among the rare percentages of men who pay for a procedure that doesn't take. He said he was happy to know that I was carrying his child. I didn't know how I felt. My youngest child was eight years old. I'd been done with diapers, feedings, colic, teething and potty training. I was sure I was done with morning sickness, swollen breasts, back pain and cravings.

I didn't want to be pregnant. Unfortunately not wanting my condition didn't make it miraculously disappear. I quickly arrested thoughts of abortion. Why do that in a loving, supportive, somewhat financially stable situation? My thoughts quickly turned to dresses again. I found a cream, lace dress, size 14, at a local bridal shop. I was going to be a mother again.

There I was checking a wedding list again, and wondering if there were less superficial things about which I should be concerned. That somber voice was speaking again, and once again I was ignoring it, in favor of the revelation that Sir Intellectual already had a tuxedo and didn't need to buy one.

Venue. Caterer. Attire. Music. Rings. Guests. I wasn't too optimistic about guests. I was sure that many of my friends and family felt they'd reached the lifetime quota for purchasing gifts and attending the weddings of the *same* person.

In all of the planning we finally talked about our future living arrangements. My expectation of having lush, new surroundings and more space was dashed. Sir Intellectual said he felt terrible that he would be moving in with us. He said his father would be so upset with him if he knew he was moving into my home instead of providing one for us. He repeatedly apologized and said he would rectify the problem in six months. I felt badly for him. I knew he was in no position to purchase a house. In the back of my mind I thought of the house in the gated community and the condo he'd talked about when we first met. What happened to them? Why was I taking the lead *again*? He moved in with us a month *before* the wedding.

The last thing on my list was obtaining a marriage license. The license clerk informed me that I needed to present my divorce papers. Sir Intellectual would need to furnish his wife's death certificate and their marriage license. We presented our papers at different times. When the license arrived, it listed my last divorce case number, but it also listed a divorce case number for Sir Intellectual. When I asked him about it, he had a ready explanation. "The county messed up. They don't even have a category for widowers, only divorcees." I didn't need to process his words. They didn't make sense even as he was speaking them. I could imagine a million referees throwing flags and blowing whistles, but I let it go. I was moving forward and the momentum, once again, ignored the voices of reality saying, "You can stop this, you know?"

15

SEEING RED

My guests at my Valentine's Day wedding were my immediate family, two girlfriends from work, and Naomi, of course. Had it not been for her Internet dating adventure, I never would have met Sir Intellectual.

When I arrived at the church, I saw my son and his family, and a church employee who was doing a sound check. I was suddenly nervous. The intensity of the red decorations matched the thumping of my pulse. There I was again. Having made sure that everything was perfectly thought out except my own feelings, I figured it was a fine time for me to trot out my list of pertinent questions. Saving face always seemed to trump turning tail, getting the heck out, and caring less what anyone thought of me. Who knows? Maybe everyone who bothered to attend my fourth rodeo would have broken out in thunderous applause if I had scooped up the hem of my dress, kicked off my heels, and sprinted to the parking lot like Flo-Jo.

I looked around for Sir Intellectual but didn't see him. No one had seen him. Maybe he wouldn't show up. For a minute I thought I would be happy if he didn't. Guests were filling up the pews in the rear. I wished they would move closer to the front and get together. At least it would have given the illusion of a crowd. I scanned the room and saw Naomi. I saw the minister as she was donning her white robe.

She began walking toward the pulpit. Candles were being lit. The clock dictated what was happening, not who was, or was not, present. A ceremony was about to begin and someone was going to get married.

Relieved, I saw my future husband walking toward the minister. He greeted her warmly. His smile in my direction was a bit fatherly and I was disappointed. I saw my daughters, but didn't see my mother or sisters. I had to put their absence out of my mind and convince myself it wasn't important. I heard the music begin. I was gripping my son's arm tightly as he walked me down the aisle. "Who gives this woman to be wed to this man?" My son yelled "I do!" then planted a rough kiss on my cheek and took his place next to his (or my family or our family) family. Everyone laughed and it was the most lighthearted part of the ceremony.

I looked into the eyes of my groom; eyes I'd looked into so many times, and saw nothing I'd longed to see. The little girl in me was doing cartwheels, and I was trying to form the words, "Wait a minute," but they wouldn't come out. I heard the words, "You can kiss your bride." It was so strange. I imagined a tornado appearing and snatching me out of the church by way of the roof.

Within seconds of even walking to the end of the aisle, he felt the need to explain to me why his friend Jamar hadn't attended. I was more concerned that *my* family was absent. I just wanted to get home for the reception and hoped they'd at least be *there*. If not for my family greeting us when got home, my sister's singing, and her mad dive to catch my bridal bouquet as if she was stealing home plate, I don't know that I would have smiled or laughed that day.

I was married.

I was pregnant.

I must be delusional…again.

I was Mrs. Gaines Hunter. My Sir Intellectual, all mine.

16

HONEYMOON

After the fourth marriage, perhaps there should be a new term for the thing a couple enjoys following their wedding ceremony. Maybe it doesn't need a special name. "Honey" implies something pure, sweet, and the result of effort. "Moon" implies something far away, mysterious, reflective, and worth exploring. Considering I was washing and drying dishes immediately after tossing my bridal bouquet, the fifteen- mile drive to the hotel didn't seem particularly honeymoon-ish. It was more like being a teenager on a field trip with a parent.

What was there to anticipate? We'd already slept together. We'd been occupying the same house for a month. We were just following the list of things people are supposed to do, perhaps just to be able to say we did it.

It's one of the many rules found in the "Little Girl Dream Book," isn't it? All weddings must immediately be followed by a honeymoon." You certainly can't say, "At home", when asked where you spent your honeymoon. Better to make up something; take a ride somewhere rather than skip it altogether. What would people say?

It's too bad that we don't consider that people aren't paying for all of the things with which we break our necks to be impressive.

As he drove, he talked about all of the things he planned to do for our family. It all sounded ambitious and contrived. (By the way, why weren't we about to board a plane or a cruise ship? Shouldn't the drive have ended in an airport parking lot?) It was quite a detailed conversation. It was the one I should have demanded we have long before we'd said, "I do."

When we arrived at the hotel the atmosphere inside and outside the car had become quiet chilly and misty. Although our room was cheerful, our dispositions didn't match the decorations at all. It seemed as if a chasm had opened up between us. There was no giddy laughing, snuggling, or frolicking on the bed. No one was chasing anyone around the room. There was no champagne or room service. It was as if we'd been assigned to the witness protection program.

The little girl inside was expecting the most magical night of her life—again. I felt as if I was sharing a room with a stranger. He seemed to reject my affection as if he was uncomfortable. We'd put the proverbial cart before the horse and extinguished the flame that comes with finally experiencing what you've been longing for. We eventually made love, but it was awkward, mechanical, cold and aloof.

Surprisingly, Sir Intellectual awakened the next day refreshed and excited. He told me that he had lots planned for me, starting with breakfast downstairs. I was looking forward to a scrumptious spread and the romantic day he'd prepared, but was quickly disappointed. He told me during our cold, complimentary breakfast in the dining room that our reservations had been changed. Our three-day stay had been whittled down to a one night stay. I knew the hotel wasn't full. There was no emergency evacuation. There was no sudden renovation project. The hotel had seemed a bit of a ghost town when we arrived. We could have had our pick of rooms. Making the reservations was the one thing he had to handle. Maybe he didn't want to spend the money. Maybe he preferred to be at home and just didn't know how to tell me. Maybe he'd planned something else during our wedding weekend and forgot to cancel it. Maybe his job had made a demand of his time. I wish he had just told me whatever it was. Sure. I wouldn't have been a happy camper, but I wouldn't have had such a miserable memory of a honeymoon night either. I *definitely* wouldn't have packed so much. A grocery bag would have sufficed. If I were going to experience sand walking hand-in-hand on the cool morning at the beach I would need to think twice because my feet never touched the sand. What was the point of taking me to a romantic location?

After breakfast, we gathered our luggage and headed to the car. I wanted to scream. I wanted to stand in the middle of the lobby and commence to having a complete, Academy Award- worthy tantrum. I wanted to press him about what happened and why. I wanted to go to the front desk and demand that the manager give me an explanation, or at least a coupon. I knew if I did, that he would have been branded a liar, or just cheap, and I would have appeared to be just plain hysterical, gullible, and fit for an asylum. I didn't want some clerk printing out proof that the fault wasn't theirs. I already knew it. The rest of our honeymoon would be spent, *not* gazing out at sunrises and sunsets over the bay from our beautiful hotel balcony, but at *my* house-- where my new husband settled in rather quickly and began claiming closet space.

17

TAKING THE LEAD

I made room for Sir Intellectual to bring what I thought were the remainder of his things. I also made room on my health insurance policy just in case he didn't have any. Too bad it didn't occur to me to ask him. My ability to confront was non-existent. I decided not to wait until I returned to work to handle it. I contacted my carrier and updated my policy to include my new husband. The whole time I felt sad that he wasn't contact- ing *his* carrier to include *me*. I had a husband, though what caliber of husband, I wasn't sure. Sometimes I wanted to slap myself for losing myself and I overlooked important things and ignored flags, bells and whistles.

I could hear my mother's voice reminding me to make sure Sir Intellectual added me to his military benefits. If anyone knew how important that was, *she* did. She had never been apologetic about making sure her daughters were well taken care of. I was slowly beginning to see her point. She reminded me of the fact that my sisters and I had never wanted for anything, certainly not basic needs, and she hadn't either. In her mind the sign of a good husband and father had little to do with romance, presents, passion, or company, but whether or not the utilities remained on, the refrigerator and cabinets were stocked, and the bills were paid in full and on time—and *her* purse wasn't ever expected to crack open to make it happen. If *she* had to pay a mortgage, be a carpenter, mechanic, landscaper, and head of a household, what on earth did she need a husband for?

My husband assured me that we would enjoy his military privileges—just as soon as he could locate his military ID. He'd packed it and it was among things he still had in storage. Every time I'd bring up the subject he concocted another excuse. First he said he couldn't find it. Then he said he didn't *want* to find it because it brought back painful memories. Finally, he said he wanted no dealings with the military, *including* accepting the benefits to which he and his family were entitled. "I've looked in every box in storage," he said. "It's just not there." In the time that passed he could have applied for a replacement, but he said doing that would be "too much trouble."

He never found the ID. We never received the benefits. He thought I should understand his reasoning and was annoyed whenever I would press the issue.

From the first Monday after our honeymoon on, he would pick me up from the military installation where I worked, and identify who he was by using his driver's license and employee ID. Here was a retired colonel subjecting himself to limited access, vehicle inspection, and scrutiny. Why?

I finally got the nerve to tell my supervisor that I'd gotten married. Instead of offering me congratulations, he asked, "Why did you do a stupid thing like *that*?" I figured it wasn't a good time to tell him I was pregnant, too.

Even as I attempted to paint a happy picture of my new husband to the few people at work whom I trusted, I had to admit that I really did not know much about him. Was his name even Gaines?

What I *did* know was that I was married, pregnant, and feeling like an idiot. I began to wonder if I was too old to carry a child to full term. I hadn't seen a doctor and had no idea exactly how pregnant I was. I hid my pregnancy at work as much as I could. Sir Intellectual was in favor of me hiding it, too. He didn't seem to want to face the music either. Buried beneath oversized shirts and winter sweaters was not only a growing life, but also growing anxiety. What would the younger women who worked at my office think of me? They'd had the good sense to protect themselves. They knew where to find pills, patches and condoms. What was *my* problem? Didn't I know better?

I had even hoped that my weight gain was a result of Sir Intellectual's cooking and my inability to back away from the table. My first visit to my gynecologist killed that notion. She was opening a practice in another state soon, but agreed to see me. Her first words to me weren't "Hi" or "Hello," but "How in the world did you get yourself *pregnant*?" They weren't exactly the words I expected to hear but that's what she said. I tried to distract her by showing her my ring, and gushing about my new husband. Why was I so eager to validate the situation by illustrating to her I was married? None of that mattered to the doctor. She saw right through me and didn't mince words about the possible complications I could face. "You are about eight weeks pregnant. There's a possibility you may not go to full term. Most of my patients who are in there forties lose the baby within eight weeks." Her voice was monotonous. She seemed disappointed in me, as if I were a child who hadn't lived up to her expectations.

She wrote a prescription for prenatal vitamins, gave me the name of a gynecologist friend of hers, and tried to smooth over her earlier declaration by telling me there was nothing to worry about.

I went back to work and passed my supervisor in the hallway. "Hmm. Aren't you too *old* to have a baby?", he asked as he kept walking. He wasn't being cruel, just giving me permission to stop hiding something that everyone already knew.

I managed to get my work done, but most of it was done through tears. I had to keep up my productivity, but I was exhausted. I was having a baby and hiding it didn't seem to matter much anymore. I needed support and strength in the worst way. I was married, but I still felt like the head of the household.

18

LOOKING GLASS

I walked into my daughter's room without knock- ing. I'd always knocked. Yes, it was my house, but she was a young lady and I did respect her privacy to a degree. I suppose the door opening startled her, because her towel fell. I saw her swollen belly and almost fainted. It wasn't the result of a huge meal. It wasn't menstruation re- lated. She wasn't just pack- ing on pounds as a result of rich breakfasts, lunches, dinners or junk food. I'd seen that belly before-- protruding from my *own* body. I knew. Our eyes locked. I could see the tears well- ing up in hers. I couldn't move. I was fighting the tears trying to fall from my own eyes. One of us needed to be strong and I hadn't exactly been successful at it for myself, but I couldn't fail my child.

She reached for her towel, fumbling as she covered herself, and stood there as if she'd felt sudden relief. All I could see was a reflec- tion of me. She had been watching me. Maybe I had made things appear to be too easy. Maybe the message I'd sent was, "Do what I do. It'll work out in the end, and if it doesn't, keep trying until it does." I knew my choices had created valleys and detours in my own life, but I thought I had successfully set up signs for my daughter to follow that would send her in a different direction. Maybe she saw me as an over- grown teenager still trying to find her way. Maybe she felt she was as adult as I was. If I could do it, why couldn't she?

I knew how nerve wracking it was to try to hide pregnancy. I knew it as a teenager and an adult. I hadn't mastered the art and, had I not been temporarily inconsiderate by bursting into her room, perhaps she would have. I didn't know my daughter was pregnant. I didn't know that she was sexually active. How preoccupied with my own life had I been that I had failed to pay attention? My daughter worked with me as a student-hire! We were together around the clock! How could that get past me?

I needed to hear what her plans were. I wanted to hear her say that she wanted to finish high school, complete college, secure a career in her field of choice, and be self-sufficient. If I had heard the word "marriage", I might have slapped myself. I didn't want to let her out of my sight. We shopped together, visited the doctor together, worked on her homework together, and cried together. It was a bonding experience, the circumstances around which I'd never wanted or dreamed, but we bonded just the same. It was painful reliving my own life each time I saw her face. "It wasn't supposed to be this way," I thought.

I reminded my daughter that she needed to contact her father and share the news with him. After cursing her, he asked to speak to me and called me a few choice names, too. In his eyes, her pregnancy was my fault. I'd been irresponsible and too lenient. I'd been self-absorbed. I'd allowed it. He was no help or support for her. He never had been. It's odd how a young daughter's indiscretion forces some men to come to the realization that the women they've hurt, used, or abandoned, referred to as "hos" or easy, were someone's daughters, *too*. It's too painful to face that you've failed to guide and protect your own. Surely someone else has to bear the blame.

The person who showed kindness and understanding to my daughter was Gaines. Somehow, his attentiveness toward her made me excuse his penchant for being misleading and evasive.

Our babies were due within weeks of one another, and Gaines did everything he could to make sure we were comfortable at home.

My emotions morphed from shame to pride as I watched my daughter struggle to continue her studies while simultaneously and preparing her world for motherhood.

I would be a new mother and a grandmother in the *same* month.

19

REPEAT PERFORMANCE

"And, who is going to give you an award for *that?*" the nurse said after I proudly declared that I had never accepted pain relieving drugs while in labor.

She rolled her eyes as if she knew I would cave soon. I felt as if I was going to die. I wasn't a kid anymore, and had to face facts. The time for making pompous declarations had come and gone. I needed the sarcastic nurse to find the anesthesiologist ASAP to administer that epidural. Two shots would have been perfect. The pain was so excrutiating that death sounded more feasible. It had been several years since I'd been spread-eagle on a gurney in a maternity ward. I didn't remember the level of pain I was experiencing. From my head to my feet it seemed as if my body was having a competition to see which joint, muscle and nerve could make me scream the loudest. I didn't have time to admire my pretty private room, or inquire about my husband's comings and goings. All I wanted was to get my new baby out of me.

Sir Intellectual was in constant motion. Anyone would have thought he *worked* at the hospital. He was very friendly with everyone and seemed to be familiar with all of the hospital staff. He just fit in and had an air of importance. He'd even crack a few jokes. His laughter was good medicine while I waited for the real drugs to kick in. Within moments, I could feel the tension leaving my body. I could not feel the contractions and the doctor even had to tell me when to push. Within thirty minutes, my son was born. The nurse cut the umbilical cord, wrapped him in a tiny blue blanket, and handed him to Sir Intellectual. He held his baby boy and stared down at him as if he was exploring the most the most beautiful creature he has ever seen in his life. The moment they took him out of his arms to weigh him, he began to cry uncontrollably, saying that I gave him the best gift ever.

The nurse handed my precious little one to me so that I could nurse him. We were asked if we had agreed on a name. I looked at Sir Intellectual and suggested our son be a junior. He said, "Since your father is no longer with us, we should consider *his* name. You always said that he was such a great man. That way you can always remember him through our boy."
So we did.

Our son was sternly looking around as if he was filled with curiosity. He was perfect and had no complications, but I suffered severe pain when I walked. I soon learned that my pelvic bone was broken. I could barely get out of the wheel chair when I was finally allowed to go home. Sir Intellectual had to carry me to the car. When we got home, he whisked me out of the truck, grabbed the baby, and got us both into the house as if we were being chased. He had prepared everything. The baby's bed was assembled and all of his tiny clothes that I bought were hanging up or placed in drawers.
Sir Intellectual took the lead with the baby while I recuperated. He cooked, cleaned and even made sure the other children got to school. Just as I was settling in to our new routine, my daughter went into labor.
Gaines immediately grabbed her bag, phoned the doctor, and rushed my surprisingly calm child to the same place I had just been three days prior. It pained me that I couldn't be with her. Her boyfriend, his mother and my mother would make sure that she wasn't

alone. Her calmness left when she got to the hospital. She'd become afraid. The contractions were coming quickly and her blood pressure rose. My mother apparently wasn't helping matters with her own anxiety. Seeing her first born granddaughter in distress brought out the bully in her, but no one was brave enough to banish her to the waiting area.

My daughter endured nine hours of labor, and delivered a little girl whose lungs were in distress. The doctors worked to clear her mouth and nose and her tiny little face soon lost its purplish hue. My new granddaughter's first bassinette was an incubator where she remained for five days. Her incessant, strong cries upon her arrival at home let us know that her little lungs were just fine.

We didn't have many visitors as we both recuperated. It was okay, though. We needed the rest. Sir Intellectual continued to tend to us all, and we doted on the new additions to our family.

October had been a busy month.

20

NEW ROUTINE

I went back to work after six weeks. My body healed and I was beyond grateful for that. I was grateful to have my mom as my babysitter, too. Even though he was in the care of my capable mother, I just hated to leave my baby. Sir Intellectual would drive me to work every morning, pick me up at the end of the day and then we'd go to get our son. Soon, my daughter would be taking my granddaughter to be cared for by my mother as well. I was so happy about the arrangement. I knew that our new babies would be loved and given all of the time and attention they needed.

I threw myself into my tasks at work. There were days when I literally lost track of time, and other days when I'd count each minute, and could hardly wait for the end of the work day. The months passed and I felt content. I began to think that I'd finally made a good choice.

On Christmas Eve, my supervisor decided to close the office an hour early. I was ecstatic. I'd driven myself to work that day. I offered a ride to a coworker, and instead of going directly to either of our homes, we decided to go to a local restaurant for a bite to eat. We chose to sit near the back of the room, ordered our meals, and decided we deserved a glass of wine, too. We chatted about everything from our jobs to our families to our holiday plans, and finished our meals rather quickly.

As we approached the parking lot, I noticed Sir Intellectual's car. I was surprised because I hadn't seen him inside. I told my coworker that I needed to see what was going on. Maybe the car had broken down there and he didn't have his phone. I suggested that she take my keys, start my car, and wait. When I walked back into the restaurant, I saw Sir Intellectual sitting at end of the bar with a woman. In my mind, I kept replaying the words he'd said that morning: "I'm going to be late. I have a meeting." All I could think to say as I approached him was, "Well, *hello*." He said nothing and continued to talk to the woman as if I were invisible. Stunned, I managed to say, "I am going to the ladies room, and when I come back, I'd better get some answers."

Every curse word imaginable came to mind. I didn't want to cry, but I was fighting back tears. I had to brace myself. My knight in not-so-shining armor appeared to have found another princess and protecting her, at least in that moment, seemed to be his priority. I didn't want to make a scene. Once again I was wishing there was a trap door I could disappear into. I thought about how my mother used to work so hard to keep up appearances. I would not let anyone see me in distress. When I opened the bathroom door, there he was, ready with an explanation. It was business. He didn't see me. She was just a friend. When he did see me, he didn't know what to say. Then he suggested that I come and meet the woman. I wasn't about to play along with him as he introduced me as anything other than his wife. I wouldn't have been able to take it. I stormed out of the restaurant, got into my car and drove my coworker to her home.

I immediately went to pick up my baby boy. I suddenly felt sorry for him. Who had I chosen to father him? How stable was *I*? I fought the urge to declare out loud that I'd made yet another mistake. As I drove, it seemed as if every voice I'd silenced kept getting progressively louder. "You don't think. You move too fast. You don't ask the right questions. You're too trusting. You're a fool. You need to grow up. You have to learn to love yourself more. You can't be afraid to ask questions and be confrontational. You can't be so terrified of being alone. Your self-worth is not wrapped up in a man." I kept repeating, "He's only two months old. He's only two months old." I just wanted to hold my baby. I wanted to imagine he was a doll and fill my mind with a perfect scenario where I could take off all of the hats I was wearing and relieve myself of so many doubts, suspicions and worries. I just wanted to be a mother and wife. Perhaps it is all I'd ever wanted.

I was so disappointed. Sir Intellectual never explained himself. I never confronted him. I was too weary to argue; too afraid to consider that my life would be changing again. I had a new baby. In my mind, separation or divorce was not an option. I suddenly felt trapped.

A few weeks later, my husband came home without his truck. He told me that his mechanic concluded that a vehicle I'd seen being operated without any difficulty on the previous day was suddenly "no good." I could think of a few other things that were no good, too, but I kept my thoughts to myself. I wondered what he had done. Had there been an accident? Had he buried it? Given it away? Lost it in a bet? Did he have it dismantled for parts? How could he just come home without a vehicle? I didn't have a problem letting him use my car as long as I got to and from work and the children didn't miss their activities. In my mind I just added the "no good" car to the list of things I wondered if he ever actually owned in the first place. I decided not to ask how much it would cost to fix it, or where it was. Once again, I simply let it go. It didn't make sense that a perfectly good vehicle would become worthless overnight, but forgetting about it seemed like a good idea. I hadn't lost anything, except periodic access to my own car when I needed it. The little girl in me was adamant that I not make waves. She needed to be happy. She didn't want any more broken families from which to recover. She needed me to believe my husband, no matter how incredibly ridiculous his stories were. It was just a car. Let it go.

21

MAKE IT BETTER

Ignoring things became routine. It just took too much energy to have reasonable questions ignored and my intelligence insulted by ridiculous answers.

I decided it was time my baby boy associate with other children. My mother wasn't happy about the prospect of one of her grandchildren being in the care of others. The daycare was costly but convenient. It was close to our house and not too far from my job. With one vehicle, convenience mattered.

Six weeks after enrollment, my son was grossly sick. His teacher phoned me with a laundry list of symptoms that demanded my attention. I contacted Sir Intellectual and asked him to pick me up. He had no job but told me he was in a meeting and was about thirty minutes away. When I hung up, I informed my supervisors that I was leaving. I gathered my things and hurried outside, forgetting that Sir Intellectual wouldn't be there immediately. He got there in less than thirty minutes, but was driving like a turtle. I was imagining the worst and praying he would speed up. I was angry with myself for not telling him to get out so that I could drive but I used that time to stay calm.

When we finally arrived, the car had barely stopped before I rushed in to find my baby. He was suffering and his entire body was extremely hot. The teacher said that he had been running around having fun with the other children during the first part of the day, when suddenly he fell ill. He smiled at me but was weak and unusually quiet.

Sir Intellectual eventually walked in and he held out his small arms to his dad to pick him up. He loved to walk and run, not be constrained, so I knew that he was feeling worse than I imagined.

I secured him in the car seat and sat in the back of the car with him. Sir Intellectual seemed to be driving a little faster and continuing to glance back at both of us. I contacted his pediatrician. The receptionist asked me routine questions. She suggested I give him some diluted ginger ale, put him to bed and call back if his condition changed.

None of the things that worked with my dolls were useful. What happened to the imaginary medicine and miraculous recoveries? The little girl in me kept repeating, "There, there, baby. Mommy will kiss it and make it better."

Mommy's kisses weren't working. I stayed awake with my son all night as the rest of the family slept.

When he woke the next day, my baby seemed to be feeling a little better. He was dreary-eyed but he was a little more talkative. He didn't want to eat. Sir Intellectual agreed to stay home with him. As I left home to head to the office, I kissed him goodbye.

No sooner than I arrived at work, the phone rang. Sir Intellectual was calling to tell me that our baby was getting warmer and may be running a fever. I headed back home and my son's fever was 104. We rushed him to two different hospitals. At the second hospital, he was admitted. He was given an IV and liquid Ibuprofen. It took no time for the doctor to tell us that my son had contracted Salmonella.

My mind was racing. His dad was just standing there, not showing an ounce of emotion.

My son was moved to a little crib-like hospital bed where he slept and whimpered and clearly wanted the IV out of his little arm.

I never took my baby back to the school. I didn't even return to get his things that he'd left behind. He got better and I was thankful. I never found out the "who" or "how" of his diagnosis. We were all so grateful that our baby was safe and sound.

22

FRAGILE TRUST

My son was two years old and still sleeping in our bedroom. He had outgrown the mini bed and the room was not large enough for the three of us. Sir Intellectual wasn't exactly happy with the arrangement and began talking about the possibility of moving to a larger house. He had been working on some private contracts that seemed to be quite lucrative.

I was still working to rebuild my credit, and it was great news to hear that he had a rating high enough for us to make home buying a reality. I was anxious to get the ball rolling and contacted the real estate agent who'd assisted me in buying my townhouse. I told her that I'd met a great guy and that we had married since I saw her last. I gushed that he was ten years my senior, very mature and smart, an entrepreneur, an architectural engineer and just an awesome person. She seemed genuinely happy for me and immediately began making suggestions.

She found seven homes for us to see. I told hubby the great news and was anxious to know just how much house we could afford. He wasn't excited at all. He told me I shouldn't have contacted the real estate agent without consulting him. Our credit scores and reports were discouraging. I know he told me his score was 750. What happened? The revelation that we'd *both* had a history of failing to pay bills in full and on time, or being overextended, didn't surprise me at all. I was becoming accustomed to disappointment however, did the report say, "delinquent child support payment?" Yes, to children I knew nothing about.

Sir Intellectual owed $12,000 in back-ordered child support. We could not buy a house, and even looking at one seemed pointless, until it was paid. Who was the child? Was there more than one? Who was the mother? Was this money owed to the adult children in Michigan or were there younger children somewhere else? Why didn't I know? No matter who it was for or how much, children come first. This was of course more important than getting a loan on a home. Who was he not taking care of?

I imagined a spirited conversation at dinner. I didn't want to deal with it though. I didn't want to hear another lie, not about something as serious as a child---or children.

I couldn't wait until dinner. I phoned him. I told him we'd received a call from both lenders, that his credit score was hovering closer to 500 than 700 and that he was $12,000 behind in child support payments. "Honey, I have to rush back to my meeting," he said. "This is all a mistake that can be cleared up with a few phone calls. I have to call you back when I am done, or we can talk about it later, but it is a huge mistake. Apparently we are dealing with the wrong lenders and they have old information on my credit report that can be cleared up immediately with one call. I have to go." Phone dead.

When I got home that night from work, he was already there cooking. He seemed happy to see me, but was preoccupied. He said he would finish making supper, leave, but would be back in a few hours. He said we would be able to discuss "the mess that the incompetent lenders put on our plates."

I wanted so desperately to trust him.

By the time Sir Intellectual came home, I was fast asleep. He avoided me for about two weeks. We never discussed the credit report. I abandoned my need to keep peace and approached him again. He had never contacted the lenders. I cornered him in the kitchen two weeks later. "Gaines, we can't avoid this conversation any longer. I want answers, and I want them now." He actually looked relieved. I don't know if he was relieved because he'd used the time to come up with another amazing story, or if he was actually ready to tell the truth. Either way, I wanted an answer. For once, I wasn't going to evade the issues. He said the lenders were lazy and incompetent and we should look for someone else. He never liked the loan guy because he was too young, eager, and inexperienced. I didn't care if he was a Martian, What did his opinion of this man have to do with the findings of HIS child support payments and low credit score? Who and where was his child or children that were owed the support?

He said that he was acquainted with a single mom who had a teenage son. She didn't know who his father was, so he started spending lots of time with him. He said he'd allowed the woman to take advantage of him and she ended up claiming her son was his. He said he never disputed it because he wanted to help the boy. He said by claiming the boy on his health insurance he became liable for child support. The little girl in me must have been taking a nap, because she didn't try to run interference.

For the first time, I asked him if he thought I was stupid. I asked him if he remembered he was talking to a woman who had been divorced three times. I knew the system like the back of my hand. He insisted that he had no clue how he landed in the child support system, but would find out the next day. I gave him the home phone that I had in my hand and told him to dial 411 to get the number of the child support enforcement office. "Honey, I know you are upset. You have every right to be, but I can assure you that I will fix all of this. It's just a simple misunderstanding."

I was growing weary of misunderstandings. I was growing weary of my own blind faith in him.

A few days later he produced a letter stating that he was not the father of the child in question and that he did not owe any back child support. I was confident that it meant we could move forward with our search for a new home. I suggested we share the letter with the lenders as soon as possible. While he was working on improving his credit score, I was paying off some of my smaller credit card debts and updating my credit report and things went back to normal, at least I thought.

I soon received a call from the lender. I was hoping it would be good news however, I was informed that the letter Gaines produced was not an original. The lender needed the original letter on official letterhead. I contacted Gaines. He said that he had submitted the original copy. I demanded that he call the child support office in my presence. He did and put the phone in speaker mode. A woman said his case was clear, and that she would send him what he needed for the mortgage loan. I was relieved, but it seemed awfully fishy that he was able to get through to someone so quickly—and who had exactly the information he needed so quickly.

I was so relieved when the loan papers were all done. There were no more nightmares about child support payments or poor credit scores, but what was required of us was more than I'd imagined. We were told that we would need $154,000, and I decided to break an unwritten rule: "Don't touch your retirement account!" Gaines said that when his business took off, he would pay me back. I was told that I would pay a sizeable tax penalty if I didn't show just cause as to why I was withdrawing the money. All I had to do was give them a copy of the contract and show where I needed to give the bank $154,000 in order to get the house. I had also written the lender a check for $6,000 as the earnest money deposit on the home. Apparently, there was no child support situation like the lady said. The mortgage guy never brought it up again. I was doing what my knight should have been doing. I was taking the lead. I was providing. If anyone asked, I would have given him the credit.

We would be closing within weeks. I instructed my real estate agent to place my home on the market. My children and I would finally have room to spread out. My son would be out of his parents' bed, in his own room.

23

UNSETTLEMENT

Sir Intellectual was unusually quiet, in fact, he was acting really weird. He volunteered to take the kids to school. When he came back, I was getting dressed. He called me to come downstairs. I asked him to come upstairs. I wanted to look just right for our big settlement day.

I asked him when was he going to get dressed. He said he wasn't. He had tears in his eyes. He said he had been pondering over the house situation for days. "God doesn't want me to buy a house just yet."

God? Had he said, *"God"?* Besides, didn't God know that he hadn't contributed one dollar to the effort? I watched him sobbing uncontrollably as if someone had died. What was *he* crying for?

It felt as if my heart would explode out of my chest. I think I was hyperventilating.

I couldn't tell if he didn't care how I felt or if he was enjoying torturing me. I had an eerie feeling that he was not only hiding something but that he truly didn't care about our family. God talks to him all the time, he said, and he told him that now was not the right time. I begin to cry uncontrollably. I couldn't move by myself! I didn't want to be separated. What about all of the other people involved at the settlement table waiting for us? The seller had just moved out to accommodate us! What would people think? My boss gave me the day off and my coworkers were planning to celebrate with me when I returned to work. He didn't care how disappointed I was. He totally ignored the children's disappointment. He was not concerned that his son was still in our bedroom. He didn't care that I might lose the earnest money and my deposit.

We didn't talk at all. I'd become accustomed to him occasionally avoiding me, but this time the avoidance was mutual. There was no communication, no intimacy, no anything. He once told me that his father had always told him, "Real men take care of family. They don't move in with women, women move in with them." I kept hearing him say that.

I don't know why I didn't just follow through with the plans without him. Why was I concerned about preserving the manhood of a man who hadn't contributed very much to the process? Then I wondered how much I had actually consulted him about his feelings or opinion. Had I just gone off half-cocked, hoping he would just go along? Did I want him to want what I wanted? Was he ready for the responsibility, or was I trying to force it upon him in hopes that he would accept it? Had I allowed him to lead? Had I made it easy or difficult for him to be honest with me? Was his behavior just a passive-aggressive attempt to get me to stop pushing and let him be the man in the relationship? I wanted space. I wanted prestige. I *wanted* a beautiful, spacious home to raise my family. Did he?

I had to focus on getting my money back. I started with the escrow account because the money was already in the hands of the seller. I contacted him on his cell phone. I started with an apology. I wanted him to know that it was my sincere intention to move into his beautiful four-bedroom, one-acre lot home. I expressed total regret that things didn't work out. He had to pay a mover to get the furniture out of the house. Our failure to follow through was creating hardship for others. I cried. "You are a kind person," he said. "I noticed you the moment you walked into my house with your baby in your arms. I wanted you to have this house because I knew you would take care of it, give it love, and restore it to the beautiful place that it once was."

THE LITTLE GIRL INSIDE

Then his tone changed. "But if you think for one moment you will make it with that so-called man you call a husband, you have another thing coming. That man doesn't love anyone except himself. He is a liar, a cheater, dishonest, and you can do much better than him. You need to leave him as soon as you can. Yes. I will give you back everything, except what it cost me to move my furniture out of that house. I'm sorry you cannot buy the house on your own. I'm sorry things did not work out." All I could manage to say was, "Thank you." His evaluation of my husband was everything I had been thinking and feeling, but was afraid to admit and accept Every word he said was true and at no point did I feel compelled to defend him.

It wasn't my place to make a man out of him. I couldn't wait for him to make the first move toward the purchase of a home. I had been impatient, or maybe I knew it would never happen and couldn't face the prospect of marking time in the same place.

The seller was trying to make *me* feel better but he was demeaning my husband, however I had to ask myself what did his words truly say about *me*? I had accepted him. I had chosen him. I'd brought him into my children's lives. I'd given him authority to treat me this way.

The little girl in me wanted so much—love, happiness, a home, family, security, comfort and luxury. She'd been programmed to believe she needed a knight to do it, but her knight had taken too long to appear, so she'd picked one. Once again she'd watch me settle for a reasonable facsimile. I'd neglected to be particular or cautious about him. The little girl would be forever linked, once again, to someone who threatened her innocence. The plan was *never* to finance her knight's armor, his sword, his horse, or his castle and be reimbursed by him later. He was supposed to approach her already suited and prosperous, with a kingdom of his own in which she would be granted a special place. She felt out of order; out of sorts. She could no longer ignore his actions, or justify her own. She had to accept part of the responsibility for the inconsistency and disappointment in her life. She had to grow up quickly or brace herself for a life of backward motion, apologies, and more tears.

24

RETURNS AND REGRETS

I decided to contact the loan company and ask for the return of my deposit. I was relieved when every cent was returned to me. I don't know why I didn't follow the receipt of that cashier's check with the rental of a U-Haul and a storage facility to move every stitch of his things from my home.

I opened an IRA account instead of putting the money back into my retirement fund. Within six months, the money was gone.

I remodeled my kitchen. I installed new floors. I bought a bed, carpeting, had the interior and exterior of the house painted, revamped the deck and landscaped the yard. I even bought theatre room furniture for the basement. I did my best to spend every dime of the money to at least feel as if I had a new home. I suppose it was retail therapy, or an answer to my extreme disappointment.

Sir Intellectual didn't say a word. He just watched our home being transformed. I would drive home after work, and dread entering, even though there would always be a hot meal waiting and upgrades were everywhere you looked. I wanted so much to end the farce that was our marriage, but the little girl in me, ever singing, smiling and clapping, wouldn't *hear* of it. Mommies need daddies to help raise the little children. Children need daddies, too.

We never talked, unless it was about the children or chores. We never had adult conversations. We did not have any type of a relationship. But did we ever have one?

Relieved to have a distraction, I agreed to allow my teenaged nephew to move in with us. Sir Intellectual helped him with his homework, went to all of his parent-teacher meetings and became the father figure that my nephew needed in his life. I admired his willingness to mentor my nephew. He'd pick me up daily from work, take the kids wherever they needed to go and run most of the family's errands. I hardly ever got behind the wheel of my vehicle and was happy that all the family could fit comfortably inside my SUV.

One evening, on our way home from the movies, the kids started yelling, "Eew, mommy, there is a condom wrapper back here, eew!" I told them not touch it. They all thought it was hilarious. I didn't. When all the children got out, I asked Sir Intellectual how a condom wrapper got into my car. I should have known he would have a ready answer. "You know how children are. It must have been your nephew. He's always acting silly. Maybe the boys were playing jokes with each other."

As usual, I kept silent. I never accused him of anything. I simply went into the house, found some rubber gloves and commenced to detail my truck as if I were a professional.

I realized that I had been doing a *fine* job of teaching my husband that disrespect was acceptable. I was communicating that I was willing to put up with anything for the sake of an intact family unit. He didn't have to be forthcoming, consistent, honest, considerate, faithful, respectful, affectionate, or responsible. I didn't expect or demand it of him. I was motivated by some strange brand of mercy. I allowed much more than I should have. I rationalized far too much. I thought the home improvements would make me happy. They were a temporary fix. There were deeper issues that couldn't be covered by a few coats of paint. The stress and effort to keep up the happy family façade was manifesting in migraine headaches. A visit to the doctor revealed I was also severely anemic. Maybe it was a relief to know that my exhaustion had an actual physical explanation and wasn't just the result of my extreme sadness and refusal to let go of all of the bitterness and disappointment I kept locked inside me.

My doctor suggested a partial hysterectomy. I agreed to go through with it. I used quite a bit of leave from work to do it. I knew it would mean financial difficulty. I didn't know if Sir Intellectual was working or not. I didn't know where his money originated or if he was forging documents. I couldn't count on him to help. I worked out a payment plan with the mortgage company and was able to apply for a modification and got approval.

Maybe it was good that we hadn't moved into the bigger house.

He was leaving every day wearing a suit, supposedly trying to get work or going to work. I decided I would get him a new cell phone. I told myself it would be my way of showing him that I had faith in him. I always hoped he would land on his feet, and for some mysterious reason, I thought a phone would help me get himself together. He was elated about the phone. What I hadn't anticipated were the emails I received because my address was linked to his new phone. The first one read:

> "If you do not come and spend some time with your boy, you will be sorry. I hate you! I thought you were coming to pick him up to meet your new wife! If you hurt my son again, you will suffer the consequences!"

At first, I thought someone had the wrong email address. Had I forgotten to whom I was married? I asked him. "Who is this woman and who is this child she's referring to?" He started babbling, so I told him to pick me up from work and take me to her. He said she was a former crack addict, trying to get her life together. In spite of all her alleged issues, he hurried to my job in my vehicle to pick me up. We got to her home in no time. She was only minutes from my job.

"Well look what the cat brought in!" she said as she looked him up and down. I smiled at her, and she asked my husband who I was. He told her I was his wife. She said, "Oh! Well we need to go inside!" I was the first one to talk. I reintroduced myself to her and said I read the emails that came directly to my email. She told me she didn't email him, but she called him and left several messages about their son. I corrected her. "You mean your son, right? She replied, "No, our son. Our son is fourteen years old."

I thought of the delinquent child support payments. Then there was the thought of the lady on the phone who said it was a mistake.

The little girl needs to hide! That trap door I'd wished would open up was elusive again. She continued. "I knew something was going on because he doesn't even come to visit. It's affecting our son in school and at home. Gaines has to do his part. He hasn't paid child support in six years!" She was talking about him as if he wasn't there. It probably wasn't hard. He hadn't been there for her. I told her I hadn't been made aware of her son. I apologized for what she was going through as if I somehow had a hand in it. She started yelling and cursing at him when I told her that he'd shared her former crack addiction. I asked her if she knew about his daughter in Chicago. She asked if I knew about his other son. That day, I learned that my son had three other siblings.

I asked her about their poor mother who died in the plane crash. She said, "Child, *pleeeeze*! Ain't nobody *died* in no plane crash! I just talked to that woman months ago! Did she die *recently*?"

We were so busy comparing notes that we didn't even notice Sir Intellectual had left the room, ran outside to either conjur up more lies or attempt to just put himself out of everyone's misery.

"Here he comes," I told her. "Child, he must know we in here comparing too many notes!" she said. We both laughed but the joke was squarely on us. He came back into the room. He seemed to be enjoying our exchange in a sick way, and we continued to give him a show. She continued to expose his lies and clear up areas which had been cloudy to me. He never said a word to defend himself or deny her accusations. There we were, having a grand time bashing an individual that both of us trusted enough to have a child with.

If either of us had been thinking, we would have rid ourselves of him long ago -- child or no child.

We were chatting like friends, but deep down we were good women who'd allowed ourselves to be manipulated by a bad person. And then there is the thought of, "well he's mine now." Why *do* women compete even when there is no clear prize in sight to win? Why do we accept suffering and dress it up in such a pitiful way? We proudly declare, "He's mine" or "He's with me" or "He was with me *first.*" Do we even bother to examine what it is we really have? How could we be so proud of such a mess? How could we engage in such a miserable game? Were we comparing to determine which of us had been mistreated the most? There we were, presenting some twisted, united front, and he continued in the knowledge that *neither* of us had ever completely exiled him from our lives and we should have completely. At what point did having *any* kind of man eclipse simply being alone? He'd never been forced to come clean and he *knew* he would be leaving with me. He also knew that the mother in me would be willing to accept his son. Our conclusion that he was sweating bullets over our conversation was woefully inaccurate. He showed no remorse.

We began to complement each other in that sick way that pretends we could make this work, for the sake of the kids. "You're too nice to put up with this." "You're too pretty. You can do better." "Good for you for kicking him out." Yet, in a disck way, we both knew at some point, we had continuously had faith that he would get his act together.

She rubbed her eyes and shook her head as we were leaving. "Check behind him, Child, because he may very well still be married to the *other* lady. There is a woman he meets up with, too," she declared. "She's a *different* one. Ask him about the woman that he was married to when he was younger! He's a big liar!"

I just looked disgustingly at the man I married. I looked at her, shook my head. I smiled, and thanked her. I didn't realize I was walking so fast. He was running to keep up with me. When I got into the truck, my head was spinning. I wanted to pass out. I had to recalculate what I'd always considered to be the first day we met. It hadn't been at the restaurant with Naomi. I was meeting him for the first time that day. I did not know this man at all.

Weeks later, I insisted that my children meet their brother as soon as possible. Sir Intellectual picked him up and brought him to our house for dinner. His child support bill would finally be paid, and he knew I would help make it happen. Saving face became a bad habit. I was determined to make it work. I actually became excited about the latest revelation. I felt maybe, bringing all the kids together would make us all closer, "the family."

We really need to replace that phrase "woman enough" with "gullible enough."

I was nursing a horribly bruised ego as the little girl in me twirled around with glee singing, "The more the merrier! The more the merrier!"

I prepared his son's favorite meal and he walked over to me and gave me a big hug. He said he had been apprehensive about meeting me and was worried I would be mad at him. I told him there was no reason for me to ever be mad. He didn't do anything. I couldn't tell him that it wasn't him that I despised, but what he represented through no fault of his own. I searched his face to rid him of any resemblance of his mother or father. He looked like an older version of my son and that made me smile. It was amazing to see them all in the kitchen together, and it hurt. My fairy tale had become more convoluted by the year.

I forgave my Sir Intelligence for the deception. Maybe I was a true Christian. Maybe the little girl had totally consumed me and my mind. Maybe I had lost my mind and it was rolling around somewhere in the wilderness. He said he didn't want to tell me about his children for fear that I wouldn't marry him. The little girl in me was so happy to hear that. To her, it meant he desperately loved me. He was afraid to lose me. I needed the little girl to shut up for a while. I needed to think. Didn't she realize non of this was making any sense at all?

I asked Sir Intellectual if he remembered that I already had three children when he met me, and he was acceptable with it. How could I possibly not accept his kids? If anyone would have been insecure about being marriage-worthy, it would have been me. Did I have more confidence than he did? Had I been as consumed with the image of an intact, prosperous family as my mother had been? Had I misunderstood her obsession with doting over my sisters and me? Had she turned her attention to us for the same reasons I had often turned my attention to my own children? Had I elevated my father to a place he hadn't deserved to be? Had I become so expert in what I wanted in a man that I couldn't recognize what I didn't want?

It had been less painful to continually focus on what he was doing to me; how he was treating me; how he had deceived me. I wasn't at all ready to examine myself. At 17, I thought I had it going on. As I aged, I kept encouraging myself that I still did. Staying married to my husband, accepting his cockamamie stories, and cleaning up his mess only proved that I didn't believe my own hype. Had my development been arrested at 17 and thrown into solitary confinement? At the end of my first divorce proceedings, had I become frozen in time? Had I emotionally matured at all? I'm afraid not.

The little girl in me was appearing to be less of an asset. With her softness, her willingness to find the good in poison, her fascination with the idea of family, togetherness, and her preoccupation with "happily ever after," she was crippling me. She wanted things now. In her magical world there was no waiting, no vetting. What glittered was gold. What people said was true. "I'm sorry," meant that everything was smoothed over, and in the wake of storms, the sun immediately returned, flowers grew and birds sang. She didn't go looking for trouble. It found her because of her goodness, but there was always someone who was suppose to rescue her. The problem was she couldn't tell the difference between the wolves and the knights. I, on the other hand, had been foolish to follow her lead.

I had been cleaning out dresser drawers and noticed that my wedding ring box was still in the jewelry store bag. I looked in the bag to ensure that nothing was in it before I threw it away. I noticed a receipt. I glanced at the name printed and signed on it. It read, "Gaines Hopper." I tucked the receipt in my pocket and threw the bag in the trash. The opposing voices in my head began talking simultaneously.

> "It's nothing! Throw it away!"
> "He's a fraud, and you're a fool if you don't confront him."
> "His handwriting is bad!"
> "Call the police, now."
> "Maybe the cashier made a mistake!"
> "You can do a background check on your computer, you know."
> "Isn't your ring beautiful? Your ring! It's so pretty!"
> "Being in possession of stolen property is a felony. You won't like jail."
> "Oh, please don't say anything! Let's sing a song, okay?"
> "Call the police and get that criminal out of your house!"
> "Maybe it's his middle name."
> "Fool! Call the police!"

I listened to the voice of least resistance and most denial. Perhaps when the salesperson wrote up the receipt, they didn't understand what my husband was saying. They should have allowed him to write his name and address on it. But there *was* no address, just the name, "Gaines Hopper," the price and description of the rings. The date was nowhere near our wedding date. I shoved the receipt deeper into my pocket.

I was already working on my masters in business and didn't want any additional information in my head. I had enough research to do. Becoming a private eye and delving into my husband's true identity wasn't going to earn me any credits or a degree. The life credits in discernment 101 that I'd been forfeiting continued to pile up in the back of my mind where I tucked away all that I knew to be true--the same way I'd tucked away the receipt from the jewelry store.

I was watching Sir Intellectual's business dealings closely. I'd believed all of his optimistic reports and inflated dollar amounts. All of the information sounded brilliantly technical and all of the paperwork he poured over seemed official. He certainly attended enough meetings in and out of town. The little girl in me popped her head out once more, and screamed, "We're going to be rich!" Money would be the answer to all of our issues. Something had to. The little girl is gleeful!

I imagined having enough money for the best marriage counselors and seven-day cruises. Maybe things would work out and we'd have the family life about which I could be proud.

When the business deals fell through, he started taking his frustrations out on me. He was a liar and a manipulator, now he added being mean-spirited and curtness to his disposition. No matter what I did or wore, he barely looked at me. He didn't care about cooking or cleanliness. He wasn't contributing financially. He didn't seem to notice when the utilities were shut off one after the other. He didn't seem to care that friends consistently helped me to restore them until they began to wonder what was wrong with me.

People don't know how to deal with you (or what to do with themselves) when the reality of a situation either flies in the face of what they have been told, refutes what they want to believe, upsets the free flow of their shady behavior, or forces them to examine the authenticity of their relationships. Living a lie is, too often, the easy way out. Lying about who's lying, and who's in the role of victim and abuser, is too.

25

NAIL IN THE COFFIN

Sir Intellectual and the guy he referred to as his business partner had been trying desperately to get their latest venture going and rebuild their cash flow—or so he said. I always wondered if it was ever going to amount to anything. Just before they'd scheduled yet another meeting with "potential investors," his partner's mother died. I thought it would be a good idea to drive to the out-of-state funeral. A part of me was actually anxious for a family outing and the funeral was a morbid excuse. When I mentioned it to my mother, I learned that she and my father actually knew the deceased. It made it a little less odd that I would be paying my respects.

As we prepared for the trip, I found out that Sir Intellectual had not one partner, but two. The second partner had been kind enough to volunteer to be an additional driver— provided we purchase the gas. He owned the largest SUV in America, a gas guzzling massive machine and, although I didn't like the idea of another person shattering my image of a family outing, at least I could get some reading done from the back seat. I have to admit it was comfortable. There was room for my children to sit on the same seat with me. Sir Intellectual took the front passenger seat. We hadn't traveled a block before they asked me for my gas card. At the gas station, he topped off the tank as his partner cleaned the windshield. They were talking so much that neither noticed the gas spilling from the tank. We rolled down the windows so that the smell of gasoline from his hands would dissipate. They thought it was funny. The men laughed and chatted like a happy couple. Sir Intellectual hardly spoke to me or the kids at all.

I dozed off and woke up as we were pulling in to another gas station. I watched his business partner lean in Sir Intellectual's' direction. He rubbed the back of Sir Intellectual's head while they both smiled at each other as if they were alone in the vehicle. The partner got out of the car to fill the tank but not before asking me again for my card. They got back in the car, acting like lovers. My husband didn't appear to notice we were still in the back seat and his partner didn't seem to care. When we got to the funeral, I wasn't sure if we had traveled with Sir Intellectual or he and his partner had traveled alone. I felt I was in a trance while sitting in the back seat with my kids. They were inseparable. I dismissed my growing suspicion until my daughter asked me if I noticed how close they seemed to be. It had always been easy for me to bury my thoughts as long as I was the only one having them. I didn't want anyone else confirming things for me, let alone my daughter. No matter what others did or said, I always knew that the hard questions would mean I had to reveal the reasons behind my acceptance of his behavior.

Of all the adjectives I could come up with to describe my mother, foolish wasn't one of them. I didn't want my daughter to view me as a fool. I hadn't exactly been helping my own cause.

We drove back and I buried myself in my books to keep from seeing anything else. I buried my suspicions. When we got back home, I once again repeated my mantra to consume myself with work. I found other things to occupy my time instead of engaging the individual with whom any interaction could quickly morph into more frustration and agitation. I hated arguing or contention of any kind--especially involving foolishness.

People can sense when you don't really want to be bothered. What they often don't want to confront is why. You work to the rule. You do everything to make sure that they have nothing to complain about.

You endeavor to make sure they can't find fault with anything. When people want something from you that you are not capable of giving, nothing else you give will be sufficient.

I tried to rest, preoccupy myself, but the somber voice returned with a vengeance.

"You may rationalize, paint rosy pictures, delude yourself, buy extravagant gifts, or work yourself crazy, but YOU got yourself in this mess. You feel it in your gut that this man is not true to you and NEVER will be. He doesn't even LIKE you. You thought you finally got it right. You are so far from the truth. This man has been witnessed calling and texting women, *sexting*, and you know he probably is sleeping with someone besides you and you have no idea whether it's a man or woman or even both! You've boasted about this man. You thought you hit the jackpot. *You've* offered to single women, "Someday, you'll find a great man." Someone like your man is the *last* thing *any* woman needs. Think about it! Either your relationship is secure or it *isn't*--and you knew full well the scoundrel you married. You knew he wasn't right! You merely *hoped* he would change. You *knew* he was a liar. He lied the day you met him and hasn't stopped since. You concluded that you had won out over all of the other women with whom your husband had previously been involved. You felt proud! You felt like you won the prize. You are correct about that for sure. He chose you alright. Sir Intellectual chose you because his primary goal in life was to always have someone he *could* manipulate--and of course, have somewhere to eat and sleep. So you didn't win anything. You were "wifey" material alright. Someone for him to consume. Take everything he could and you allowed it to happen. You are playing with fire. Has it even ever occurred to you he could bring home a disease? What about an incurable disease? You ever heard of HIV? Do you realize what you are doing? How you are jeopardizing your life, your family? Is he even paying one bill in your house? He's probably staying in there for free? What were you thinking? No, why weren't you thinking?

You should have held out for genuine, authentic love, and respect. You valued HIM more than you valued yourself. Now you have a dog on your hands, and will spend your entire married life being suspicious and stressed every time he walks in or out of the door. Your friends can't help you out of this mess. In fact, no one can but God; but you have to take the first steps. This man is your problem. You knew better. *Yes,* you did. Stop shaking your head. You know you knew better! Yes, you did! You just *chose* to ignore your own intuition, and not believe your own eyes. That's why it is so important to love yourself, *first.* Pay attention to what's going on around you. Address the REAL problem. Don't ignore it any longer than you already have. Make sure that what goes on behind closed doors is real, so you won't spend so much time fabricating bliss to mask what you don't want others to see.

I didn't want to hear it. It hurt so badly. I had to literally slap myself out the trance! The little girl inside of me began waving balloons. She wanted to celebrate. In fact, I did, too. My baby and granddaughter would soon be graduating from nursery school. That became my focus. I had to put the energy back on my children. I focused primarily on the kids because I needed to exert my attention some place other than myself. I wasn't feeling too proud of myself at all. I needed a diversion, something that makes me happy.

I got a call at work from the school. My son's tuition hadn't been paid. There would be no graduation. Sir Intellectual only had one bill. Tuition was HIS responsibility. He'd said his "jobs" would take care of it "until he got back on his feet." I forgot I was in my office and burst into tears. Out of the blue, a friend called. I could barely get the words out. "He didn't pay the tuition! He promised he would!" My friend told me not to worry. He rushed to his credit union, and then drove to my job. He brought me a cashier's check, told me to get in his car, and he rushed me to the daycare center to pay the bill so that my baby could graduate from kindergarten.

Sir Intellectual said that the director must have not kept good records, because he paid her on time, every time. He said she was a ruthless, unorganized person who had been attempting to wreak havoc in his life. I wanted to tell him that he was a ruthless, unorganized person who had successfully wreaked havoc in mine, but of course, I didn't.

My son and granddaughter graduated from kindergarten. They both sang in the adorable program their teachers had planned. My granddaughter's father and his family were there. Also, Sir Charming (yes, my ex-husband), he came too with HIS family. It was a little awkward for me. I couldn't help but wonder, "Did I go further backwards?"

Sir Intellectual was the picture of the doting father. He even hugged the director. I guess he wasn't repelled by her wickedness after all since someone else paid the nursery bill.

26

RETREAT

Isn't it amazing how challenges can send you running back to church? It's the last resort in a long line of attempts to repair what keeps breaking.

I'd heard about a spiritual retreat for women and decided to go. Maybe if I got away from my family, I could hear more clearly what I probably already knew—and act on it. I would be free of computers, phones, and distractions. I'd never met so many women who were so knowledgeable of the Bible. I was fascinated by the way they could complete the facilitator's sentences because they knew biblical scriptures so well. I hadn't been able to retain much of anything. There were too many competing voices in my head.

I wasn't even worried about leaving the house in Sir Intellectual's care. I just wanted to go. I completed everything I had to do at work, turned over assignments to my co-workers, and asked family to look out for my son. I packed sweats, oversized shirts, and one dressier outfit for the concluding service. I was happy to have someone offer me a ride for the two-hour trip. Rev. Hannah had been my confidante but I never shared with anyone how this man lied. She wasn't a meddling woman either, but God-fearing. She knew there were problems in my marriage, but she never gossiped or prodded me for information. Somehow I always felt as if she had been praying for me.

We rode in silence for a while, and then she said, "You're worried aren't you?" "Worried about what?" I asked. She said that she could feel the tension when Sir Intellectual and I had arrived at her home that morning. She felt as if he was hiding something from me. I didn't take offense or try to be evasive. I could feel the tears welling up in my eyes."Rev Hannah, Gaines has been hiding something from me since day one."

"Well, Darling," she said while driving, "We're going to pray right now," as she reached for my hand, "that you get to the bottom of the secrets! You need to be free. I bet you also think he may have homosexual tendencies too, don't you?"

I snatched my hand away. I was suddenly afraid. "How did you know I thought this?"

"I got my ways of knowing things, but the truth is it's *obvious*. You're just too close to see. God is going to reveal to you on this retreat whatever it is you need to know."

She grabbed my hand again and began to pray:

> "Father, in the name of Jesus, I honor you. You're trustworthy and faithful. You're merciful and kind. Thank you for being there; for hearing me. Thank you for this opportunity. Your daughter is so full of doubt. She doesn't know what she has gotten herself into. She has forgotten how to love herself. Give her clarity, knowledge, instruction, guidance and all the awareness she needs, not just about her husband but about herself. Do not let her go another day without opening her eyes--fully. Be there for her. Comfort her, God, not only when you reveal the truth to her, but when she finally accepts it."

When she released my hand, I felt like grabbing her hand again and holding onto it tightly. Being in the company of a trustworthy, God-fearing person was refreshing. She smiled and continued driving.

"God is going to show you something beyond your wildest imagination. Just wait and see."

When we got to the conference center, a pleasant woman gave us our admission packets. I was happy to be there.

All of the ladies were greeting each other as if they were long lost friends. Any embrace left me teary-eyed. Their tight, sisterly hugs and smiles seemed to squeeze the problems out of every pore and let me know just how wounded I was. I needed to cry.

I met my very soft-spoken roommate, and headed to the elevator. I couldn't afford to have a room to myself, so I opted for a roommate, even though I wasn't too keen on sharing a room with a stranger. Based on how I was feeling, however, anyone would do as long as I didn't have to deal with the demands of home or work.

My roommate put her things away and left the room. I remembered Rev. Hannah's pattern of prayer and prayed myself. I remember saying, "Father, I do not know what is happening but I feel you working already," as I rose from my knees.

I shed my black attire and put on something pink. I decided to walk around the grounds of the conference center. The azaleas and roses were so beautiful. I knew it was time to find the dining room for the opening session. I didn't feel like sitting with strangers. I didn't feel like talking or answering questions either. My quiet roommate was nowhere to be found. However I was compelled to sit with strangers. It was someone in that room that I was supposed to sit and talk to that I had never met in my life. I walked right over and decided to join an elder who was sitting by a window. She motioned for me to sit down before I asked if it was okay. She introduced herself and I found out that she would be one of the facilitators. I told her what an honor it was to meet her. She stopped in the middle of enjoying her salad, put her fork down and said, "Young lady, God is watching over you. My ex-husband used to lie to me all the time, too. I later realized it was a sickness. It was never going to stop. To keep it from affecting our children I knew I had to leave him and I did."

She picked up her fork and took another bite of her salad. Had I been eating anything, I would have choked. Was she some kind of mind reader? Had someone told her to be on the lookout for a sad woman dressed in pink?

"I know what you are thinking" she said. "How does this old woman know so much about what is going on in my life when I didn't tell her anything?"

I smiled embarrassingly and nodded in agreement. It was exactly what I was thinking."You're on your way to becoming a nervous wreck," she said. "After a while, you have to stop being a victim."

She told me that my husband had kept something very important from me that would either make it easier for me to remove myself from the marriage, or, he would simply remove himself.

I'd only been there less than a day and was already feeling lighter. Perhaps I just needed someone else to tell me what I already knew. Maybe the little girl in me needed permission to be silent.

Every speaker seemed to echo the same sentiments:

> Be honest with yourself.
> Stop lying to yourself.
> Stop trying to mask the real issues with clothes, jewelry, and make-up!
> Stop comparing yourself to other women.
> Focus on spiritual fitness as much as you focus on physical fitness.
> Surrender every problem to God and have faith that
> He will never forsake you.

Each time I went back to my room, I felt as if things at home were miraculously changing. I didn't sleep much. My mind was cluttered. I didn't want the experience to be some temporary emotional high. It was empowering being among the women that weekend, but how would I fare when it was over? What could I learn in one weekend that I hadn't learned in several years? I had to remember that I wasn't there to acquire tools to fix Gaines. I had to admit there was something damaged in *me* and my focus was to make the first step within myself to fix what was broken.

When I arrived back at home, I was barely through the door before I calmly asked, "Gaines, what is it that you want to tell me?" That wasn't exactly the right question. He didn't want to tell me anything. But, I should have asked him, "What is it that I'm about to find out about you?"

It was as if I had catalogued every lie he ever told me and every person associated with them. I would be getting answers about them all whether I wanted to hear the truth or not. Whether I got the answers from him, or not, didn't matter. I wasn't merely going to be set free; I would be made free. I'd learned that I was the only person blocking my freedom.

I went to check on my son, prepared for bed, and decided to phone Naomi. She didn't even say hello. "What'd he lie about now?" I didn't really know yet what to say so I politely told her that I would call her later. I needed time to think, not chat on the phone with girlfriends. Sometimes, that can only make things even worse. I had all the information I already needed. At least, I felt I did.

At work, the Monday morning after the retreat, I thought back to the conversation I'd had with his other son's mother. The somber voice spoke again. "You're not legally married."

His wife was alive. His children were alive. He had not one grown child, but two—adults--a boy and a girl… He had families in Brooklyn, Greenville, and Detroit with whom he had cut ties. There had *been* no plane crash. No divorce. The only person he'd told the truth about was his father. His father not only missed him but was also ashamed of the person his son had become. He was also very protective of his first daughter- in-law and his grandchildren. To him, I was just one in a long line of gullible women who had assisted his son in shaming his family's good name.

I walked into the house that evening to the aroma of lasagna. The little girl in me immediately began boasting what a good cook he was.

"Don't be mad. We could go to Detroit, and all of the other places and make everything go away, come back home, and have a big pretty wedding and a party!" We could make everything all right!"

I had to shut her up once and for all. I commented on how good the food smelled, because it *did,* and then I asked, "What has happened to you? Why do you feel you have to lie *so much?*"

He put down the spoon he held and shouted, "Honey, I told you I divorced that woman in Massachusetts!" It was as if he'd been waiting for me to ask, but his answer shoved me into reality. If I had any thoughts of remaining in denial, they left immediately. All of sudden, his dinner *didn't* smell so good. Who'd said *anything* about Massachusetts? I was inquiring about the long lost family members he had, period! "Your wife isn't dead. You have family. Why lie about it?" He just looked at the floor and said, "She was dead in my eyes. They're all dead in my eyes. I came here to start over." *Really?*

The ringing of my phone startled me, but I didn't initially answer. I didn't want any more distractions or excuses to walk away from an important discussion. We just stood there in silence. Another ring let me know a message was waiting. I felt an urge to hear my message. *"I hope you're sitting down. Your husband not only has a wife in Chicago, but he has a former wife who currently lives in your city with her new husband. From the address, it appears she's a few blocks away from where you live. There's more but I don't want to do this over the phone. Give me a call back if you want me to forward the information. I'm so sorry."*

I left Sir Intelligence in the kitchen. I rushed to my bedroom, closed the door, and locked it. Sir Intellectual had never been violent. I'd never been afraid of him. I don't know why I locked the door. I'd never felt imprisoned in my own home. I should have though. This is just as bad. I had to tell someone what I'd just heard. My own friends might not be inclined to be sympathetic. I don't know what made me phone his son's mother. Maybe I needed the support. Maybe I felt her misery needed a little company. Mine sure did.

"Child, *pleezze*," she laughed. "I done told you that the only kind of news you are going to get concerning him IS *disturbing*! Ha! I done told you girl! That man ain't right!"

I don't know if she was laughing at me, him, or the fact that I'd had the nerve to phone her. She seemed to enjoy giving me details and I continued to listen. I figured I might as well let her get it all out of her system. I suppose it's nice to have someone believe you are not exaggerating and can truly relate to your bad experiences. She could.

I couldn't believe how calm I was after the conversation ended. Maybe I'd cried so much that there was no emotion left. "It's over," I said as I entered the kitchen again. "You have to go." He didn't become belligerent at all. He just said he needed time to pack and "gather his thoughts." I told him I would happily pack his things *for* him but he had to leave my home that night and "gather his thoughts someplace else." It wouldn't be much effort for me to pack his things, because he only had clothing and a fake HD television—that came from the storage unit where his military ID was supposed to be.

I walked back into the kitchen and insisted he leave immediately. He resurrected a few "Sweethearts" and Darlings" that I hadn't heard in ages. He tried his best to persuade me to allow him to stay. He tried sympathy. "I'll be homeless!" I was sure it wouldn't be the first time, and a liar like him wouldn't be out of doors for long. I needed him gone. He needed to be out of my hair for good.

He stayed outdoors on the porch until someone eventually showed up to get him. I didn't peek outside to see who it was. I didn't care if Santa Clause picked him up. He had to leave. I just wanted him and his lasagna gone.

27

SIGH OF RELIEF

Prayer works! If you don't pray, surround yourself with others that pray until you do. The retreat was a weekend of spiritual healing for me. No more fairy tales although as Dorothy the good witch says, we have the power all along. Yes, I did, but not until I grew up and took control of my own life.

I felt relieved. I felt like a steel beam had been lifted off my back. I couldn't dwell on how naïve I'd been. It was important to acknowledge my hand in my own pain.

My rolling stone knight in shining armor had left me alone, a loan, in debt, and an engine problem in my truck. I didn't care. There was no amount of detailing or repair work in the world to help me rid myself of his shenanigans. I had to budget like a miser, but I bought a new car. I didn't want any tangible reminders of him. The retail therapy was just what I needed.

He was gone. The heaviness in the house was gone. My dislike of myself was gone. The rooms seemed brighter; bigger. The little girl in me was sad for a while until she heard the word "party." She hadn't grown up an inch, but I was nearing 50 and in need of a celebration so that I could bring in my birthday with all of my friends as well as a time to celebrate my freedom, not just from Sir Intelligence, but from repeating a viscous cycle.

A friend helped me to retain an attorney. Another friend helped me get caught up with delinquent bills. Yet another paid the attorney's fees. It's amazing how many people are poised to help you as soon as they see that you mean business and start helping yourself. Not even friends are eager to help you finance and maintain a mess, but they will certainly help you to get *out* of a mess.

I was hurt, embarrassed, and betrayed. I felt somewhat sorry when I heard that Gaines was homeless. For a moment, I considered it was my fault. But I got over that thought quickly.

I didn't want to trust any man ever again. Although men were everywhere, and temptation was too, I had to modify my behavior. I had to trust myself. I'd always had a man in my life, or at least someone looking in my direction. Having a man in my life could no longer define me. I suppose my neediness was shooting off of me like sparklers on the Fourth of July. For once in my life, I had to forget about who was looking at me, how handsome or well-heeled I thought they were, how long it had been since I'd been admired, and focus on getting my life in order. I couldn't continue to allow my brokenness to attract broken people who threatened to reduce me to irreparable pieces. I had to understand that everyone who wanted to be with me was not "The One." Everyone who flirted with me was not an answer to my prayer. I had to position myself to be healed and then loved I couldn't help the process along by catapulting myself onto the back of every seemingly trusty steed that rode by.

28

OWNING IT!

"You can scratch *this* marriage off the list," The judge told me. "It's null and void. Madam, I do not understand why people don't take the time to seek a divorce before they marry someone else. It affects so many families and it's more prevalent now than it has ever been. I'm surprised to see as many cases as I've seen just this year alone. It's making no sense to me, but I'm sure you're relieved to know that you are now a free woman. Your marriage is annulled!"

His words stung a little. The way he'd emphasized *"this marriage"* let me know that he had some knowledge of the other three. I had to bind and gag the little girl inside. I became hurt and embarrassed again at the mere thought of four failed marriages, but then I immediately looked at the bright side. I was free. In her mind, "free" meant getting coupled up again. She didn't know how to be alone and was afraid. But I did. I became smarter and wiser. I was looking forward to finding out where I'd left all my sense of being.

Two years later I thought it was safe to enjoy the company of a man again. I didn't see the harm, but I was channeling what I was not familiar with, all of my turtle and snail tendencies. I completed my MBA. I enrolled in a class to help me manage my finances. I stayed as busy as I could. I couldn't just say I was working on me; I had to accomplish that mission first and foremost.

Sir Intellectual can visit our son as much as wants to. I forgave him as well. My son loves his father. I'd always felt that children couldn't ever get too much love. If he grew up and arrived at the conclusion that his father was a jerk, it would be his own opinion, based on his own observations and experiences, not mine.

I joined a local church. I realized I needed to stay connected with God. Because he saved my life. I needed to understand *his* brand of fatherhood and true love. I needed guidance in how to establish a real relationship with Him. I began to surround myself with people who were at least *trying* to live according to God's plan. I wanted to understand the Bible *myself* and not just be in awe of people who seemed to be scholars at comprehending the Bible.

On one particularly quiet evening, I sat down and scribbled a list on a legal pad:

1. Always pray, first and foremost!
2. Give freely.
3. Don't abandon your standards.
4. You can't control what another person thinks.
5. With the right listener, you don't have to repeat yourself.
6. Take the time to get to know people.
7. Time, love, and money can be stolen. Don't allow it.
8. Don't be so needy.
9. Don't think more highly of yourself than you ought to. Be humble.
10. You are worthy because you are created by God.
11. No compromising, especially if it means loss of self-worth.
12. Be honest with yourself.
13. Your internal presentation has got to improve. What's on the inside will radiate on the outside, no matter how cute you are.
14. Being a go-getter can have its drawbacks. Slow down.
15. You chose to be deceived. Don't do it again.
16. Remember your children are always watching you.

17. Forgive, so that God will forgive you.
18. Always practice honesty with God. He knows the truth anyway.
19. You are no better than anyone else. Never lose sight of that.
20. Stop focusing on material things. They neither define nor exalt you.
21. Listen more. Talk less.
22. Stop looking for potential in others and identify quality you can see today.
23. Everyone is anointed to do something.
24. Stop being a people pleaser.
25. Don't be afraid to fail. After failure comes success, just not in *your* timing.
26. Joy trumps happiness.
27. Go back and discover where and when you stopped loving yourself.
28. Be grateful. Always have in the forefront your blessings.
29. You can't hide how you really feel about yourself.
30. Pamper yourself in good times and bad times. You are still a rose.
31. Smile, even when you want to cry.
32. Cry when you have to but get over it.
33. Make sure your heart and mind are in sync when making a major decision concerning your life.
34. Don't spend too much time harboring over past mistakes.
35. Move forward.

The little girl inside is still chattering away. I listen to her chatter sometimes and let her play. She's not all bad, but she can't be allowed to direct or influence anything anymore in my life. She stopped maturing long ago, but she is exactly who she is supposed to be. To maintain her ideals and follow her lead, however, is to continually allow myself to be hurt. She's always looking for someone to rescue her, protect her, and provide for her. Her choices aren't always the wisest. It's okay to want peace and happiness. It's okay to see the beauty in everything. It's not okay to lose yourself in a realm where lies reign and deception. It's funny. The people we're so concerned about wanting to please are probably not interested in us anyway. They usually have their hands full tending to their own affairs of what is most important to them.

Until we see ourselves the way God sees us, we will forever be connecting with others that are as broken as we are. It may sound selfish but we can only fix ourselves. If we don't be careful, we will continue to repeat the vicious cycle and believe their lies, make excuses for what should not be defended, and accept what should be hastily rejected.

At seventeen, something in me was frozen in time. For years, I operated and thought as that teenager. Her issues had never been resolved. I repeated her mistakes. I kept using her methods. She'd experienced a warped version of love and didn't know how to free herself or heal from its effects. She was still on her fairy tale mission.

I had to stop listening to her whether she was six or seventeen years old. I was now a grown woman.

There's something about the little girls inside of us. They only know how to go backwards or mark time. They don't have to grow up. It took a while, but I realized that it was past time that I did.

Perhaps there is someone else with whom to share my life, but it won't be out of necessity, insecurity, desperation, or loneliness. I will no longer be expecting another person to complete, mend, save, or validate me. If I am going to be happy, I will not have to wait for someone else to ignite the happiness. That's my responsibility. I have to reflect on my life and hold myself accountable for my own actions. I had to own my role in my own pain and deal honestly with myself. It's a continuous effort. It is after all, my life. I have to own my role in my own pain.

WHAT'S HAPPENING NOW?

Things are going extremely well. The little girl inside of me still has a place, to ensure I have compassion for others however, that is her only role. I no longer try to implement the perfect family and give my children a father figure. When I have those thoughts, I ask myself,"Do you really think a perfect family exists? I now know the answer to that question, and no longer spend days/nights searching for it. The difference today is, I don't worry about what I lack, and I treasure what I have. It has taken lots of pressure off of me. I believe my family is happier as a result.

My children are all doing well. I am grateful to be their mom.

The little girl inside of me is quiet now. She has a tranquil spirit and is content just where she is - where she is supposed to be. I'm running the show for me, seeking God's blessings over every move I make. I'm simply making better decisions concerning my life. I use the discernment God has given me over my life.

On the relationship-front, I've been in a five-year, "stable" relationship. The "M" word is not our focus. We are savoring each moment we spend together by simply getting to know one another. There is no rush! There is no since of urgency. What's the rush? The best thing a person can do in a relationship is to spend enough time together to determine what it is they don't like about the person they are interested in. Then ask yourself, "Can I live with this person and put up with what I don't like about them for the rest of my life? If the answer is "no," please, run!!! And most importantly, never go into a relationship with plans to change a person. Don't reason with yourself that they have "potential." Because what happens if they never reach their potential and frankly, who are we to dictate someone else's potential? Consider whether you can love this person whether they live up to their full potential or not. God blessed me with a partner that respects and appreciates me for who I am, the complete package-the good, the bad, and the ugly (what he may not like). I am forever grateful that I did not give up on love. My single friends, love is out there! Don't ever give up on love. And, in spite of it all, you are still a rose!

Love yourself and embrace your mistakes and learn from them. Keep smiling and be grateful. It starts with you taking the first step to own up to your own pain. God will help you from there.

Stay tuned for the "*whole* story!"

ABOUT THE AUTHOR

Tonya Barbee never dreamed of writing books but she's always enjoyed telling stories and sharing profound testimonies. This is her first project, with another one underway. She's excited about encouraging others, particularly women, to find their way during transgressions and to never, ever, give up, no matter how challenging the journey may be. She lives with her two youngest of four children in Bowie, Maryland and works in Washington, D.C. as a Project Manager.